AF326799

The
Broken Election

Second Edition

The Broken Election

By

Scott Gulbransen

Visit the Sear Press Website at **www.searpress.com**

Published by Sear Press
PO Box 2294
San Diego, CA 92192

2nd Edition published 2004
by Sear Press

ISBN 0-9749264-1-8
(Previously published by Counting Coup Press,
ISBN 0-9708598-6-4)

Printed in the United States of America

For Alexis and Ryan
You both are the light of my life.

Table of Contents

April 2004

Four years have passed since I penned The Broken Election during that fateful winter of our discontent. What started out as a simple project to journal my thoughts and feelings to pass down to my kids became a book that I stand proud of even today. Is it a great piece of American prose? I can't say for sure but I can tell you that the people who have read it – of both political persuasions – tell me it moves them closer to understanding what was at stake for many of us during that tumultuous time.

The 2000 presidential election, in many ways, has never ended. The nation today is as divided now as it was then. The fundamental differences between the two major political parties continue to be light years apart and the upcoming election will undoubtedly be as close as 2000 was.

The first edition of this book was released just a few days prior to September 11, 2001. That day changed America forever and changed me forever. The terrorist attack on our own soil reunited the nation – albeit for a short time – and seemed to heal many of the wounds inflicted during the broken election of November 2000. For perhaps the only time in the last decade, Republicans and Democrats rallied behind our president during a time that challenged the resolve of all Americans.

In many ways, the events of that day, and George W. Bushs' leadership after, seemed to validate what I wrote during election 2000. I had said, in my own partisan and emotionally driven way, that Bush was a much better leader for our nation than then vice president Al Gore.

I shudder to think about September 11th with Al Gore sitting at 1600 West Pennsylvania Avenue.

Clearly, history proves Bush was up to the task and was the right man for a trying time and led us into our current war on terrorism. The war on terrorism, declared just after September 11th, is a war with no end in site; a war unlike any we have ever face; a war of good against evil and tyranny against freedom. President Bush has led this nation bravely into this fight.

The nagging question is: three years later is Bush still the best man for the job? As I write this new introduction, peacenik and Jane Fonda protégé John Kerry is the Democratic nominee to run against Bush in November 2004. Kerry is as liberal as they come and don't necessarily represent the views of Americans but he will have a chance to beat Bush this coming fall. As of early summer, Kerry was holding on but not by much. His flip-flop on about every issue important to American voters - from abortion to the funding of our military - continues to dog him. Unless the war in Iraq continues to produce the number of U.S. military casualties as it did in April 2004, Kerry may be a long-shot.

Why is my confidence in the man I wrote so glowingly about just under four years ago shaken? For whatever reason, President Bush has decided to adopt several policies that have alienated his core Republican and conservative voters.

First, as was widely speculated in 2000 when Bush first ran for and won the presidency, the president in January 2004 introduced his new policy for allowing amnesty for the estimated 10 to 12 illegal immigrants currently in the United States. As someone who has written a book about our porous borders and the threat they pose to our national security, this was a complete shock. The immigration issue killed Gray Davis in California and led to a sweeping Arnold Schwarzenegger victory and the advent of the "Governator." It could bring Bush down in November ushering in another eight years of Democratic rule and ruin in Washington.

The second Bush misstep involved something less substantive, yet telling about where his agenda is headed. Bush, as part of his fiscal 2005 budget, is rewarding the National Endowment for the Arts with an $18 Million increase in funding. For unabashed conservatives like myself, the NEA is about as close to the poster child for government waste as you can get.

The NEA is the organization that funded such valuable projects as paintings of the Virgin Mary covered in dung and a crucifix depicted in a jar of urine.

The fact Bush is willing to spend my tax dollars – and yours – on vulgar displays of "art" doesn't make me feel warm and fuzzy about him. In fact, I am pretty upset about it.

We're told constantly that Bush is a conservative yet he has grown the government and our nations deficit continues to balloon. Frankly, his budgetary prowess is frightening and I am concerned it could cost him and the Republicans the White House if he doesn't reverse course.

Conservative Republicans in America are nervous about their president. It appears Karl Rove, Bush's most trusted political advisor, may be leading the president down a path that could have him a "one and done" president just like his father. At a February 2004 meeting of Republican leaders in Philadelphia, conservatives blasted Rove and Bush for their stance on immigration and the failure of the president to "prove" he is a conservative. This includes his support for a Constitutional amendment banning gay marriage.

What is certain is Bush is his own worst enemy in 2004. Will he stand up for what he truly believes?

Either way, America is again in for a long and hard battle. It makes many of us long for the days of our greatest modern president, Ronald Reagan. There was no doubting where Reagan stood on the issues. It's about time George W. Bush looked to his father's former running mate for the inspiration to do what is right.

Election 2004 could be as acrimonious as 2000. My question is could this nation handle another protracted presidential election during a time we are at war?

I am not sure we can but let's hope Election 2004 isn't a replay of 2000 - the broken election.

Scott Gulbransen
May 14, 2004
San Diego, CA

Introduction

November 7, 2000, is a day that will be studied by historians ad nauseum. That day, which started out as a standard United States presidential election, would leave in its wake a slew of historical events no Hollywood scriptwriter could have penned.

This book is one American's experiences and thoughts about the political process that suddenly found itself under the world's microscope. My purpose is really rather simple; I started a journal so the memories would never fade and could be shared with generations to come. I had thoughts of sitting in a rocking chair telling my grandchildren about the election and what I was doing during one of the most trying times in American history.

As I thought about it more, I decided to put my thoughts and experiences in a more permanent record that is this book. The first chapters give a glimpse of why I am a staunch Republican and the experiences that led me to vote for George W. Bush in the 2000 election. This sets the table for November 7, 2000, and why I felt as I did in the weeks that followed that historical vote. My hope is anyone who read this, from my family members yet to come into this world, to the stranger who finds themselves reading these pages, have a better idea of what people were thinking and feeling during this tense, frustrating, emotional and pivotal time in the history of the greatest nation to every grace the face of our Earth.

My expectation is that not all of you will agree with my views and that's fine. What makes our nation so great are those very differences and the passion each one of us share as it relates to the direction our country takes each election day. Love or hate my views, I hope at least my experience will lead to further discussion of the election of 2000 and why it was so divisive.

ONE

History 101

In everyone's lifetime there are moments in history that stick out a bit more than others. There are personal moments like the birth of a child, your wedding day, the day you graduated high school and college, the death of a loved one and your first kiss.

Those moments are indelibly written in our mind and everything that we become in life can be traced back to moments such as these. I remember so vividly my first professional football game in 1975 when my father carried me through the parking lot at Arrowhead Stadium in Kansas City to see the Chiefs play the mighty Pittsburgh Steelers. We sat in the upper deck and I remember being cold and more interested in the vastness of my environment than what was happening on the football field.

These personal memories are very important to me

but I've always had a true sense of history and a keen feel of truly historic moments. I remember having the chicken pox. I don't remember them because they itched or because I was very ill. I remember them so well because I had them on the 4th of July 1976. While my family barbecued in our massive midwestern backyard, I was quarantined inside the house watching images of bicentennial fireworks taking flight over the Statue of Liberty. I remember being in awe of the moment even though I was merely seven years old. As I itched the red bumps that enveloped my skinny frame, I thought ahead and wondered if I'd be alive in 2076 to watch the United States celebrate it's 300th birthday.

There were other moments in history I can remember so clearly if I had any artistic talent I could paint a portrait. One of those moments was January 28, 1986 while in the 10th grade I was attending my Spanish class when the school public address system crackled with life and readied for an announcement.

"My I have your attention please," said Dale Mitchell, vice principal at Carlsbad High School. "I regret to inform everyone at Carlsbad High School that just few moments ago, the space shuttle Challenger exploded on liftoff from Cape Canaveral, Florida."

The rest of his word's I don't remember. As a patriotic

young man, and a space shuttle aficionado, my body tingled as I felt my scalp recede and my hair stand on my arms. The lump in my throat swallowed hard and made a noise I can still hear today. This was a national disaster for my generation.

I read many things about the 1960s and the civil unrest. I listened attentively to my father tell stories of the night Martin Luther King, Jr., was assassinated and how he found himself in a prominent black neighborhood in Chicago as rioting enveloped the areas around him as he made sales calls. But stories are stories. I felt a disconnect; as a child of the 1970s, I experienced no civil unrest or war on the evening news. Things were rosy for my generation.

But the Challenger disaster was one I could call my own. I am not romanticising it but it is the truth. Most friends I talk to today can remember where they were and what they were doing when the Challenger climbed ever so high only to fall to Earth in such a disastrous display. It's much the same when I talk to my parents and they recall exactly where they were when president John F. Kennedy was assassinated on November 22, 1963 in Dallas. They were both defining moments two separate generations could not forget.

But just 14 years later, all Americans were about to

witness an historical event that would surely change us all forever.

TWO

My Political Journey

Since turning 18 in 1988, I had never missed voting in an election. The Constitutional right afforded all Americans was important to me. It was something instilled in me at an early age by my parents. Since both were just one generation removed from immigrants, my parents always talked about how important it was to vote. I listened for 18 years and exercised my right to vote in 1988 when I voted for George H.W. Bush who became our 41st president.

I even worked for President Bush when I volunteered to work on his campaign in San Diego County. I was determined to be an active part of the election process and support the candidate I felt best represented the population of our country.

Bush had no problem beating Michael Dukakis and the Reagan ear lived on with his less than exciting vice president taking over where he left off. I still believe Bush was a good president but he did make some fatal flaws and the Republican Party had become complacent. For nearly two decades they had their way building our military, helping temporarily to end the threat of Communism worldwide and pushing conservative values through various programs. Coming from a family where my father was very conservative and my mother a liberal conservative, I had chose to go the direction of my father and from an economic standpoint agree with the platform of the Republican Party. I always viewed the Democrats as a free spending bunch who really had the interests of minorities and the bottom end of the economic food chain as their main battle cry. I came from a white, upper middle-class family so I found it very hard to related to the issues that separated me from my Democratic brothers and sisters. But as I grew older, graduated high school, and started college, my views would change leading me down a different path.

The early 1990s were a confusing time for most young people. Our economy was not as strong as it once had been and our national debt continued to rise as a direct result of military spending and more attention spent concentrating on foreign relations when things were bad at home.

Being a college student still in search of what I was

and what my long-term goals were, politically I gravitated toward the left. As with most young college students, I was experiencing new thoughts, new people and building a new morality that led me away from the conservative views of my childhood and towards a more Democratic position on most issues. I blamed my woes and inability to secure financial aid for college on the Republicans and President Bush. I couldn't get a good job to support myself during school and my increased agitation with "the establishment" grew. I began exploring the civil unrest of the 1960s including a lengthy study of the Vietnam War. Even though my generation had never experienced our peers dying in a war or the strain it put on our nation at home, I felt obligated to fight the powers that be and live my life differently.

I remember at the same time having conversations with my father as it related to race relations. Around the same time, the Rodney King incident sparked national outrage with cries of police brutality and rampant racism. My father, who had experienced a stabbing at the hands of a black man, held some views that I felt, at the time, were racist. I remember a discussion of the Rodney King incident that became inflammatory and led to a large confrontation between us.

"As far as I am concerned, he deserved it," my father

said of Rodney King. "Typical. A black man claims racism after he broke the law and now he wants people to feel sorry for him. He should be in jail."

"Dad, how can you say that? They beat the guy for speeding. I don't care if he was wrong or right, no human being deserved to be beat like an animal."

"Give me a break. The guy was speeding and what if he would have killed someone else? He didn't give a shit. He's a piece of human garbage and they should have finished the job."

"That's a racist viewpoint and it's those white officers that are human garbage," I screamed back.

These types of exchanges were commonplace during this time. I truly believed in the civil rights of all Americans no matter what their color, religion or sex. My father, jaded by bad experiences as a youth, could not see that. His years of resentment toward one person were manifesting themselves in a very different way. At the time I just resented his close-minded opinions, later, I would realize it he was simply a product of his environment as a youth. Did it make his opinion right? No would be my answer but as I matured, I learned to respect his opinion because as Americans, everyone is entitled to an opinion no matter how wrong we may feel it is.

One night, after drinking rather heavily with some friends of mine, I came home and found my father still awake. I was very emotional having recently broken up with a long-term girlfriend and having lengthy discussions with my other liberal friends at a local pub. I remember feeling as though our generation had no future. The current leadership of the country seem so far removed from me and I broke down in tears.

"I'll never be able to buy a house or enjoy the rewards of life you and Mom have been able to," I said to my father.

"Scott, that's not true. You're young and that's why it's important for you to finish college," my father said. "Things will be fine."

Although I appreciated his words of encouragement, I did not believe things would be fine. My feelings of despair and abandonment seemed to be common amongst my generation and my circle of friends. I had the gut feeling our nation was heading in the wrong direction and needed to be shocked.

As things began to look up for me, I had been accepted as a transfer student at the University of Nevada, Las Vegas, the country was gravitating toward a new man. His name was Bill Clinton and he was the Democratic Party's' candidate for president in 1992. I started to feel better about the nation and was in favor of a change. I even changed my part affiliation when I arrived in Las Vegas and became a registered Democrat.

Bill Clinton was an appealing candidate for young people. He was a master at telling us everything we wanted to hear. Hell, he even went on the Arsenio Hall show playing the saxophone. What 20-something voted wouldn't vote for the first true Rock-n-Roll generation candidate? Bill Clinton spent more time on MTV in 1991 and 1992 than Madonna or Mötley Crüe and we were all wiling to follow this Pied Piper into the White House.

He was cool to George H.W. Bush's' wimp; he was the Beatle to Bush's' Lawrence Welk; he was oil and Bush was water. That sharp contrast was what America was waiting for and most of us were willing to overlook his obvious failings just for a fresh start.

As charming and big brother-like as Clinton was, I could not find myself comfortable enough to vote for him. There was something in his eyes I couldn't trust and he didn't earn my vote in 1992. Some of my conservative economic values still held their grip on me and the only candidate I could punch that hole for, was, Ross Perot. In essence, I was still disenfranchised and my vote for Perot was more of a vote for "none of the above" than a tacit vote of support for the crazy Texan.

Needless to say, Clinton easily won in 1992 under a mantle of improving the economy and gaining more rights for gays and minorities. His first move in office was to try and force the U.S. military into a pro-gay policy that soon backfired on him but would not stop the Clinton Cannonball from blowing apart his opponents. The Democrats loved Clinton as much as the Republicans had loved Reagan. The difference was Clinton had wider appeal and his views were centrist and socialist in nature. People liked that but I didn't. Soon after he was elected, I began to run toward my conservative past. Something was telling me the Clinton vision for America was not the most prudent and I wanted no part of it.

THREE

The Elephant Beckons

In 1995, after graduating from UNLV after almost six years in college, my life changed dramatically and so did my political views. After spending the past 4 years in heavily Democratic Las Vegas, where labor unions rule like they did in the 1950s and 1960s, my views had become more conservative.

I had met Eliete Muniz, the daughter of Cuban immigrants that fled the island nation after Fidel Castro led his successful revolution, and was convinced she was the woman I would marry. I began, for the first time in my life, to think about starting a family and buying a house. I looked at my liberal past as just that – the past. I had gay friends, friends who were very "live for today" and didn't give much thought to moral or religious values. But my future wife and I shared the same conservative roots and we found ourselves returning rapidly to those roots.

My later college years had moved me back to the right. I wrote from that point of view in The Rebel Yell, the student newspaper at UNLV. My most famous column, during my time there as Opinion Editor, was a piece I wrote on Olympic swimmer Greg Louganis. Louganis had come out to say he had contracted HIV through unprotected sex with another man.

The fact that Louganis was gay was no surprise but his series of interviews with various national television shows struck a nerve with me. Louganis, in my view, was asking for pity from America. It seemed as though the bright young man wanted all of us to feel sorry for him. He also seemed to be taking the position as spokesperson for the gay movement as it related to the fight against AIDS.

My personal views on gays had no bearing on what I wrote. My column, written quickly and off the top of my head, created a firestorm that would find me a target of groups bent on pushing their own agenda.

The gist of the column was this: have compassion for Louganis as a human being who has contracted a horrible disease but don't feel pity; he after all made the conscious decision to have unprotected sex with another man. In the same column, I wrote of recent AIDS victim Eazy-E. Eazy-E was a rapper with the infamous NWA gangster group from Compton, California. He had died shortly before Louganis's announcement. Eazy left behind a young child and I called for my readers to feel sorry for the child orphaned by this awful disease, not Louganis – an adult who made a terrible lifestyle choice.

After the column ran in our normal Thursday edition, I was swamped with phone calls and would soon learn something that would truly disturb me. A group of gay students reproduced my picture from the column and hung posters all over campus with titles like "UNLVs Admitted Gay Basher," "Straight From the Gutter," which was a play on the true title of my column, "Straight From the Gully." I received death threats on my message machine at the paper and a request for an interview by the local gay newspaper The Bugle. I knew going in the interview would be slanted and meant to paint me as a bigot. Luckily, being a reporter myself, I would not give them the "smoking gun" they were looking for. The story was actually pretty even but one of the paper's columnists painted me as a frustrated homosexual who was afraid to come out of the closet. Luckily, I found the humor in that.

What this one incident did for me was show me

freedom of speech and the freedom to express my views as a journalist was under attack. The new sensitivity that had swept our nation under the Clinton administration was taking on a life of it's own. Suddenly, if you had a strong opinion that anyone could misconstrue as "insensitive" (by the way, the word "insensitive" means nothing. Another liberal invention so they can call you a bigot without proving it!), you were labeled and bigot and ostracized. I refused to accept this and all it did was move me further toward my conservative past.

How was such a small majority of people in our democracy was wielding so much power? Let me say, I believe completely in the civil rights laws we currently have on the books. But since when did the rights of smaller groups mean the majority must be subjugated to ridicule and the very same labels these groups were established to fight? If gay and minority groups live under the impression that we can all be impartial and "just get along" all the time, they are living in a fantasy world. This became apparent to me quickly but I wasn't willing to give into the pressure.

Fundamentally, I believe much of this movement is a direct result of the crumbling structure of the traditional American family and the movement of the Clinton administration. I have no problem with gay people serving in government or doing any job. I would fight to the death the right of any American, whether straight, gay, Christian, Muslim or Jewish, to be afforded the same rights under our constitution. But, in my opinion, because of Clinton's desire to please these fringe groups, he appointed minorities and gays to his cabinet and other key federal positions because of their color or sexual preference. In my mind, that is as bad as discriminating against them. This type of pandering is what led me away from any of my Democratic views and I began to rapidly return to my Republican roots.

FOUR

Time For A Change?

The 2000 presidential election was important to me. I had followed its developments since 1998 when political pundits first discussed possible candidates to face vice president Al Gore. Gore, who was by his own admission unexciting, seemed to be on the ropes despite the popularity of Clinton and the booming American economy.

The 1998 sex scandal involving Clinton and former White House intern Monica Lewinsky, led to impeachment hearings in both houses of Congress and many people lost faith in the president. Despite his attempt to hide the truth, which included lying directly to the American people on several occasions, Clinton survived as the underdog from Arkansas again convinced the American people he was sorry.

Despite graphic accounts of Clinton and Lewinsky engaging in oral sex in the oval office, and the president lying under oath during depositions, Americans still supported their president to the tune of a 63 percent approval rating. Clinton had disgraced the office of the President and people seemed to not even care. It seemed as though the economy and personal prosperity and made Americans immune to even their own morality.

The good news for Republicans was the Democrats were perhaps vulnerable on this front. Most conservatives felt come November 2000, the Republicans would have a chance to win back the White House. Since people were happy, employed and making tons of money on Wall Street, the Republicans had to look for any way possible to break the Democratic leadership hold on the land's highest office.

The man they selected was George W. Bush.

Bush, not exactly a Ronald Reagan himself, had wide support throughout the party and journalists and political observers started calling him "the anointed one." Before he even announced his candidacy, it seemed most conservatives were in agreement that Bush was the best choice. Being the son of former president George H.W. Bush, "W" was a feel good candidate who was charged with leading us out of, what I call, The Eight Years of Darkness.

Bush seemed a solid man with good views, if you knew what his views were. Early on, I think many Republicans had trouble relating to him because they didn't know his stance on the issues. In retrospect, being a public relations professional myself, this was a brilliant piece of strategy. The earlier Bush addressed the issues, the earlier the Democrats would have to attack him and build their case for Gore. Still, many were uncomfortable with Bush and many looked again to Colin Powell. Powell, former head of the Joint Chiefs of Staff under President Bush, was the popular man most wanted to run. But for personal reasons, Powell had resisted in 1996 and again in 2000. Many people believed it was due to his African-American heritage and the possibility of assassination. I believe Powell just didn't want to subject himself or his family to the scrutiny that comes with the office.

Bush announced in he would run for President on June 12, 1999, at a speech in Cedar Rapids, Iowa. It came as no surprise but still I needed some more convincing. During that speech, Bush made some points that really hit home with me. He said:

> "I'm running because our country must be prosperous. But prosperity must have a purpose. The purpose of prosperity is to make sure the American dream touches every willing heart. The purpose of prosperity is to leave no one out... to leave no one behind.

I'm running because my party must match a conservative mind with a compassionate heart. And I'm running to win.

Prosperity is not a given. Some in this administration think they invented it. But they did not invent prosperity, any more than they invented the Internet.

Governments don't create wealth. Wealth is created by Americans — by creativity and enterprise and risk-taking. But government can create an environment where businesses and entrepreneurs and families can dream and flourish.

We'll be prosperous if we reduce taxes. I'll have a plan that reduces marginal rates to create jobs, but a plan that also helps struggling families on the outskirts of poverty. I believe that after we meet priorities, all that remains must be passed back to Americans, so it will not be spent by Washington."

Bush's message rang true for me. As an educated professional, I was by no means at the poverty level but like most Americans was a few paychecks away from it. I owned a new home and had a good job. Yet my taxes were high and I was being punished for being married and having a working spouse. The year I bought my home, 1999, my wife and I made a nice living yet with the deductions for interest on our mortgage, and the standard deduction for our daughter, we still had to pay the IRS at the end of the year to a tune of $691. Now, I understand that's not a ton of cash but for a young family that's almost a mortgage payment.

The Democrat's talk of tax cuts for the middle class was hollow in my eyes and I couldn't figure out why more of Americans couldn't see it. With consumer debt at an all-time high, it seemed most of Americans were happy with their material possessions and the sense that everything was good in our country. Bush said over and over again, we needed prosperity with a purpose. It seemed our prosperity in 1999 had no purpose. I believed Bush was the man to bring us that purpose.

Like most Americans, I did not agree with my candidate on every issue. Bush called for normalized relations with China. I felt normalizing anything with the most powerful Communist nation on Earth was a bad idea. China's human rights abuses coupled with their ability to man an army of 200 million raised a flag in my mind that had huge letters saying caution. Americans seem to live today under the false assumption there are no countries who pose a threat to our national security. When the Berlin

Wall fell, we all got very sentimental and embraced the Russians and eastern Europeans like nothing had happened. I agreed with most of it but there are still forces out there who want to see our system and way of life fail. One of those forces is China.

Despite my disagreement on that issue, most of Bush's other positions I back completely. It was with great optimism that I began contributing to his campaign and looked forward to the day when I could enter the polling booth and vote for him.

Bush's only serious challenge within his own party came from Arizona senator John McCain. McCain, a decorated war hero who was a prisoner of war in Vietnam, was energetic and had ideas about reform I liked very much. He dubbed his campaign bus "The Straight Talk Express" and began winning over Republicans and Democrats with his talk of campaign finance reform and middle class tax cuts.

At times, he and Bush seemed to attack each other personally which hurt the Republican cause overall. And, despite some key victories in a handful of states, Bush prevailed and eventually won the support of Senator McCain. Perhaps out of desire to run again in 2004, McCain did not seem to really work tirelessly for Bush on the campaign trail. He did his best but I wondered if that was his decision or the Bush campaign to keep him a bit on the quiet side. Whatever the answer, Bush now had the complete support of the Republican Party and the strategists took aim at their own White Whale – Al Gore.

FIVE

The Calm Before the Storm

October 2000

The last of the three presidential debates completely solidified in my mind that George W. Bush was the best man to lead our nation into the new Millennium. Bush seemed to be on an upswing that might take him straight to Washington. Although the popular polls gave Bush the lead by just a few percentage points, conventional wisdom said he might win the popular vote but Gore could pull the desired Electoral College vote to win the White House.

My personal fear was that exact scenario coming true: Bush takes the vote of the people and Gore wins because of the large states giving him a slew of Electoral votes. But I had a gut feeling as Halloween rolled around that Bush and the Republicans would prevail. It may have just been wishful thinking but I could feel the national making a turn.

November 2, 2000

The news broke and suddenly my stomach felt empty. A 24 year old driving under the influence ticket became public knowledge and suddenly George W. Bush was in trouble.

Bush had apparently been pulled over during a visit to Kennebunkport, Maine, in 1976 and had been issued a citation. This news spread like wildfire and screamed of grandstanding by the Democratic Party. Although the Gore campaign completely separated them from the source of the story, most people believed they had some part to play in its release just days before the election.

But a piece of me wasn't too worried about this revelation. If Clinton could perform a sexual act with a cigar in the oval office and be forgiven for it, certainly the American people wouldn't let a 24 year-old incident change their mind on who should be the next president.

Was it wishful thinking again? Sure. This time, it turned out to be true as most people when asked about it dismissed it as a mistake from the past that should remain in the past. Still, there was no denying the release of the information had hurt Bush. How much it would hurt him was the question of the hour. We would have to wait until Election Day to find out.

November 6, 2000

Early in 2000, I had come to know the owner of an upstart Internet news site. The syndicate, named *The Strategic Jungle Syndicate*, was born out of disgust for the mainstream media and their overwhelming liberal bias. Besides being faltered and excited about the offer, I was thrilled about the chance to again write opinion columns, especially on the current political events.

As we approached Election Day, I was a bit nervous and was losing confidence that Bush could pull out a win. The driving while intoxicated conviction Bush had been cited for in 1974 was in the news and no one knew what effect, if any, it would have on his narrow lead in the polls. In a column I wrote on November 6, 2000, I discussed the problems conservatives faced in modern America:

More Persecution for Conservatives Awaits

Here we are on the eve of perhaps the
closest presidential race in over 60 years
and it appears Democrat Al Gore will win
the White House ensuring another four
years of large government intruding in our
lives.

Before you curse me for giving up before
the first vote is cast, hear me out. No one

wants the Republican candidate to win more than I. A true, dyed-in-the-wool conservative like me wants nothing more than the Clinton-Gore age of terror to be over. Eight years of bickering and egotism like nothing this nation has ever seen before has taken their toll on this young man.

But if you look at all the signs around us, to be labeled a conservative in today's American society is equivalent to sewing the scarlet letter right smack in the middle of our chests. Our liberal opponents will rush anytime we speak of conservative values to tell us we're "hate mongers" or "insensitive." It's amazing to me that if you believe in a traditional family or state that you believe homosexuality is morally wrong you're suddenly evil.

In a society where we must now watch every word we say for the fear of being branded insensitive, how can conservatives survive?

This presidential election has been a microcosm of the trouble conservatives in America face every day. Gore, as exciting as watching mud dry on a Tennessee riverboat, constantly rails against the conservative right and their desire to cut government spending and provide tax relief for families throughout America. The one message he echoes over and over again is that Bush really wants to give the largest tax cut to the wealthiest one percent of Americans.

Besides being false, Gore's assertion implies it is bad to be wealthy. The last time I checked, in a free-market economy, the goal was to work hard and amass an estate to pass on to future generations. Do

you mean to tell me that the everyday
worker in America, perhaps the attendant
at a McDonalds near you, doesn't desire to
move their station in life? Are they content
at their $7 an hour job as long as the
government provides ssistance?

The answer of course is no.

Why else would gambling and state
lotteries be so popular if people in this
nation didn't want to be wealthy? Again
Gore feeds on the fears and jealousy of
Americans to trick them into thinking
being wealthy and conservative are bad
things.

Whether it's abortion, gay rights or
Medicare, the conservative view is being
silenced by a select few who want to push
their agenda on the rest of us. To think Al
Gore is not a rich boy who came complete
with a silver spoon in his mouth is naïve
and apparently America is ready to believe
it.

Yet the conservative mantle has rekindle
the thoughts of many Americans. How else
could you explain the neck-and-neck race
with the incumbent party? In many ways,
Al Gore should be mortally embarrassed.
He talks so much about American
prosperity yet most Americans don't buy
into it enough to hand him the election by
a landslide. The truth is, Americans are not
enjoying this prosperity as much as Gore
would like us to believe. Instead, the vice
president's wealthy friends in China,
Russia and Hollywood continue to
bamboozle the populous into thinking
they're better off than they were eight
years ago.

All the people need to do is look at their

consumer debt, condition of our schools,
our healthcare system and the moral
crumbling of our families to see the true
legacy of the Clinton-Gore regime.

It's a tough time to be a conservative in
America. Much like Christians in ancient
Rome, we're soon to be thrown to the lions.
It's unfortunate but at least Al Gore will be
entertained.

This column, written just 24 hours prior to the election, truly captured my state of mind. The election was a make or break for most American families and I could sense that. I received email from many of my readers saying I had "given up too soon" or was "letting the Democrats scare you into thinking we won't win." Whatever it was, I had a huge mix of feelings – some good and some very bad.

SIX

Surprise, Surprise

November 7, 2000

The morning of November 7, 2000, was a chilly one in San Diego. I awoke to find my wife and daughter slumbering next to me in our bed, my thoughts quickly wandered to the election. I watched my daughter Alexis sleep and I wondered if when she awoke the next day we'd have a Republican president; a president that cared more about protecting families and moral values than bowing to the Hollywood elite. As I watched her tiny face, I said a prayer and began my day.

As significant as Election Day was to me, I was still a registered vote in Nevada. I had sent my absentee ballot weeks earlier so my vote for George W. Bush was already in. I carpooled with my father that day and his excitement was evident.

My father's excitement was almost childlike. We left at 6:30 a.m. and drove straight for the polls.

"I've waited eight years for this day," he said. "Let's leave early so I can stop at the polls."

My father's desire to vote for Bush was dampened a bit when he found the poll closed.

Alas, he had arrived too early and would have to wait until after work. That meant I would have to take the train home and would have to wait to hear election results. I felt like a sports fan waiting for the big game.

Throughout that morning, I checked almost every 15 minutes to see if any early results had come in. It was the first election in which I had unlimited access to the Internet and I kept checking everything from CNN.com to ABCNews.com. As much as I wanted to find out who would be the next president of the United States, it would be later in the day to hear some good news.

At about 3:30 p.m. (PST), I heard the first results come over the radio inside my office. Bush had jumped out to an early lead by winning some smaller midwestern states. I was cautiously optimistic about the results but I truly believed Bush was on his way to victory.

All day, reports that turnout was larger than expected

was good news. In an election with so much at stake, I was happy more people were exercising their rights. Even if the vote had not gone the way I wanted it to, early on it appeared more people were taking part in the process.

The fact that so many people fail to vote completely shocks me. Millions of Americans have died on the battlefield and in the streets to ensure the right to vote and still so many turn away. Most blame it on voter apathy saying people feel disconnected from the political process and thus don't vote. I personally have a problem with people who constantly complain but refuse to do anything about it. One vote does matter and most of the public was about to learn that in a big way.

4:42 p.m. (PST)

As I waited on the platform to take the commuter train home, discussion of the election was everywhere. San Diego, being primarily Republican country, was full of Bush supporters. Bush-Cheney bumper stickers seemed to be as chic as Internet stocks were just a year before. The professionals, who ride the train home, expressed themselves in various ways as they checked the election results via their cellular phones.

"Finally we get rid of these scumbags," an executive type in a business suit said.

"Gore's as stiff as a dead man. I can't wait for January 20th," another man who appeared to be a computer programmer.

Hearing all of these conversations made me feel good. I had a false sense of security and began to think Bush really would carry not only the popular vote but the Electoral votes as well. In wanting to win, I had lost my sense of reality for just short period of time.

5:06 p.m.

The train pulled into the station and I hurriedly jumped off and set out to look for my wife who was picking me up. The day had gotten blustery with the threat of rain sweeping in over the Pacific Ocean.

As I climbed into the car and kissed my wife, reports on the radio reported that Gore had closed the gap to within two Electoral votes.

"Damn!" I exclaimed.

"Bush is still ahead but they said he might take Florida real soon and he already won Michigan," Elie said.

"If he takes Florida, then it's over. I can't believe the people in this country are so fooled. I'm depressed now. I thought Bush was really going to win."

My desperate talk led to my wife patting me on my

knee and giving me a look of sympathy. Elie had seen my interest in the election and the passion I felt for Bush and his candidacy. As we drove to McDonald's to grab some dinner, the disappointment was draining me. Always a competitive person, losing bothered me. I started to come to grips that Bush might lose and all but reserved myself to the fact. Since I was a young boy, I always employed a tactic in which I would admit to loss or accept defeat while in my mind thinking it was the opposite. This time, I truly felt the battle was lost.

5:43 p.m.

Upon arriving back home, I immediately spent some time with my daughter in front of the television watching election results on CNN.

The first comments I hear, declare Al Gore the winner in Florida and my mood again turned for the worst. CNN quoted Voter News Service; a national service that monitors exit polls to determine winners, as saying Gore had carried Florida. This was bad news and all Republicans could hope for was a surprise somewhere.

Within about 20 minutes, good news began to trickle in. Bush had taken West Virginia, a traditionally Democratic state, and was starting to string together an impressive collection of Electoral votes. As Bush gains momentum, and barely after I could digest my meal, my man was making an impressive run. The TV talking heads started to pick up on Bush's gain. Some were even going as far to say that even if Gore carried California, as he was expected to do, Bush's strong showing may be too much for the vice president to overcome.

That was just what I wanted to hear. My mother and father were both home and were watching the election results with us. My mother, Cassandra, a jack-Democrat, also supported Bush and so we were a unified household as we hunkered down to watch the results on our television screens.

6:55 p.m. (PST)

As Elie and I continued to watch election results pour in, a shocking development occurred. Suddenly, CNN's Bernard Shaw looked flustered as the camera closed in tight around his face.

"We have to apologize but we're now taking Florida from the Gore column as the vote there makes it too close to call," Shaw said with his face almost turning red.

For the first time in my lifetime, I had seen a state awarded to a candidate taken away because the vote was too close to call. Besides the obvious embarrassment this created for the networks, a collective cheer from Republicans all over the country could be heard. I literally heard cheers up and down our obviously Republican street. Suddenly Bush supporters felt the White House was within our grasp. I remember thinking that Bush only needs three or four of the larger western states and toss in Florida and we would have an Electoral College landslide.

"Thank God he's going to win," I said prematurely to Eliete. "It would be great if he somehow carried California too. That would kill Gore."

I was gloating and loving it. I started to move around the house a bit more and do some laundry while still keeping an ear to the television. Eliete was nine months pregnant so the anticipation of the arrival of our son Ryan was first on my mind but the election had captured the attention of everyone in the house.

As the states started lighting up behind the various news anchors, it became evident the race would go down to the wire. Most agreed that it might be early in the morning before America could learn who its new president was. The anchors on CNN, Bernie Shaw and Judy Woodruf, looked very tired as the race moved into the morning hours on the east coast. As the anchors complained about their long hours, the tide was definitely in favor of Bush. Most "so called" television journalists, who had earlier in the evening almost declared Gore the winner of the White House, now were echoing my wishes – it appeared Bush would prevail. The western states were about to report within one hour and everyone knew Bush would win most except California.

As a former print journalist, and a true believer in the journalistic ethic, this night was the first time I could see plainly how slanted the media truly was – particularly television. Respected journalists including Dan Rather at CBS, Tom Brokaw at NBC and the aforementioned Bernard Shaw at CNN, all tipped their hat to their own political views and those views bubbled to the top.

The confusion set forth by false projections by both Voter Monitoring System and the major television networks most likely discouraged some voters from making it to the polls and would be the topic of discussion for weeks to come. Either way, it had everyone sitting on the edge of his or her seats. I was no different and was fixated on the results trickling in on my television.

10:30 p.m. PST
Despite the closeness of the race, and the fact Bush and Gore were tied at 242 electoral votes, I decided to leave the

television on and try to get to sleep. I kept my ears in tune with CNN as I kissed my wife and set my alarm for 5:30 a.m. for work the next morning. But it was a fruitless endeavor.

I kept tossing and turning hoping to hear the news I wanted so badly to hear. I wanted Bush to win and was hoping he could somehow pull out the victory late in the game. It became evident soon after I laid down for my slumber, the whole ball of wax depended on Florida. Whichever candidate could win the Sunshine State, would be the 43rd president and the most powerful leader in the free world. It was a true case of irony seeing as Jeb Bush, George W. Bush's younger brother, was the governor of the state and had promised his brother victory. As I started to doze off with CNN blaring in my ear, I wondered if I would awaken in a country with renewed leadership.

11:15 p.m. PST

The memory is fuzzy.

I remember rolling over on my back and realizing I must have been asleep. The long day at work, coupled with the strenuous election return monitoring had taken its toll on me. As I rolled over and rubbed the confusion from my eyes, I looked to the television screen still shining light in the black room. Not two seconds after I turned my attention to the screen, CNN came back from a commercial break and declared George W. Bush the winner of Florida and the winner of the 2000 Presidential election.

I quickly nudged my wife.

"Elie? Bush won. He won. Thank God he won," I said.

As my wife jumped up from her slumber, she gave me a hug and simply said "Alright!"

I suddenly felt a surge of energy. My emotions ran wild throughout my body. I watched the joyous celebration from Austin, Texas, I felt as though a huge burden had been lifted from my soldiers. In my opinion, the election was a pivotal point in our country's history. We would either continue our dangerous, morally bankrupt journey down the path forged by Clinton/Gore or find our way back to the true path that only Bush could steer us down. It appeared, thanks to Florida, the Clinton nightmare was over.

As I paced throughout the house in my underwear, I continued to raise my hands in the air as though I had just secured 1600 West Pennsylvania Avenue as my own home. That's how important it was too me. I then slowly made my way into my daughter's room and sat next to her watching her peaceful sleep. I made the sign of the cross over her head and said a quick prayer of thanks to God for helping Bush prevail.

Bo Derek and Wayne Newton were partying in Austin in front of the Governor's Mansion and things were good. It was surprising to me since most of Hollywood's elite crowd were staunch Gore supporters.

I picked up the phone and talked to my father about what we all felt was a victory for America.

"Dad?"

"Hey, I've been waiting for this for 8 years," he said.

"No kidding. Now maybe we'll all get a tax break." I said.

"Alright son. I'll see you tomorrow."

"OK. Bye Dad."

Elie was nine months pregnant and had already fallen back to sleep once I returned from my phone call. I wanted to celebrate with someone but the family was asleep so I just watched the reaction. CNN flashed to the scene in Nashville where the Gore supporters all stood shocked and silent waiting for their drone of a leader to concede the election.

Bush had won and for the first time in a long time, I felt my voice had been heard.

11:30 p.m. PST

"We're told here in Nashville, Bernie, that the Vice President has just called to congratulate Governor Bush and has conceded the 2000 Presidential Election. His top aides tell us Gore will come to the Memorial here in Nashville to offer his concession speed and thank his supporters. We're told that will come in the next hour or so."

Those words, spoken by CNN correspondent John King, offered some finality to the battle. It was a battle for the White House but for many conservatives like myself, it was about sending someone to Washington to right our country's path.

Of course, I couldn't sleep. I decided it was worth a sleepy and exhausting day at work later that morning in order to enjoy the sights and sounds of the first true political victory I felt a part of.

I watched with excitement as the anchors desperately tried to fill time until Al Gore arrived to finally bow out gracefully.

"Where the hell is he," I muttered in the dark room.

Of course the real reason I didn't go back to sleep was I wanted to see Bush speak and share in his victory. I had contributed to his campaign and I wanted to go to bed with some real positive images in my head.

Every channel I turned to was filled with images of Gore and Bush supporters in their respective states. It was now five minutes until Midnight and Gore still had not arrived. I felt somewhat angry that he was late and wasn't conceding in a timely fashion. But something in my gut told me there was something amiss. Something was wrong and no one could really figure it out.

November 8, 12:00 a.m. PST
The television screen flashed again and a startled Tom Brokaw came on the air.

"We're told that Vice President Al Gore is now en route to the Memorial to give his concession speech," he said.
I ran downstairs and grabbed a Diet Pepsi. My throat had become dry in all the excitement so I quickly grabbed a cold can and returned to our room. It was almost a euphoric feeling as I chugged the cold soda and watched the TV with excitement. I had sort of tuned out the commentators and just watched the images.

What struck me was the crowd at the Gore rally. Most were younger men and minorities with some women scattered throughout the crowd. Part of me felt sorry for them. They were obviously passionate about their candidate like me but now they had to give up hope and face reality. I looked upon them with a dose of respect and then let out a cry of joy.

"Yeah! No more Gore!" I said aloud. There was no one to hear me since my wife and daughter were both sleeping but it just happened.

Some 10 minutes later, Gore was still nowhere to be found. Although the networks had reporter a few minutes earlier that Gore had arrived, he still hadn't made his way to the stage. CNN and Fox News both reported that Gore was indeed there but no one knew what he was waiting for.

12:41 p.m. PST

What was going on? Gore still was nowhere to be seen and none of the networks knew what was happening.

Then, like a brick hit me square in the eyes, CNN reported the news.

"We've just learned from our contacts inside the Bush camp that Vice President Al Gore called just moments ago to retract his concession. Apparently Gore aides believe the vote in Florida is too close to call still and they believe they may win the state and in turn the White House."

The words of CNN correspondent Candy Crowley left me speechless. In this seesaw battle between Bush and Gore, the results were still in doubt.

But how could that be? Every network proclaimed Bush the winner. How could Gore concede and retract? This had never happened before. The election was as close as they come but no one, I mean no one, had an answer for this bizarre turn of events.

My heart sank. I could not believe that the election was now in doubt. The thoughts of Bush being our next President suddenly faded from my head and all I could feel was worry, anger and uncertainty.

This twist was unparalleled in modern election history.

In 1960, the election between Richard M. Nixon and John F. Kennedy was so close many cried foul. Mayor Richard Daley of Chicago, a politician like none we can find today, allegedly stole the election for Kennedy by turning up "missing" ballots in a precinct in Chicago. Those votes gave Kennedy the White House and he went on to become one of our most beloved Presidents.

The discussion of 1960 had been at the forefront of many conversations throughout the 2000 election because everyone knew it would be a close race. But no one could have projected the election night drama that had unfolded in front of Americans. Television had brought the election to us in real-time but on this night it added to the confusion and would continue to play a part in the unfolding drama in Florida.

Once hearing Crowley's report on CNN, after pinching myself to make sure I wasn't having a nightmare, I gave my wife a shake.

"Elie? Wake up! Gore retracted his concession. Can you believe that?"

"What? What are you talking about?"

"They are saying now Bush has only a 300 vote lead in Florida. They're going to wait until the morning. This isn't right. Something is up." As I gave my wife a hug, we watched on through the night before retiring at 4 a.m. with less answers than we did the previous evening. We were supposed to have a new President. Instead, we were about to be plunged into a crisis the nation had not seen in over 100 years.

SEVEN
The Morning After

November 8, 2000

Uncertainty is something Americans have never liked. In a technologically drive modern society, we had become accustomed to instant information. Whether it was via cable television or the Internet, American's appetite to know the latest news about everything from movies to election results fueled the confusion of November 8, 2000.

As many Americans turned off their alarm clocks and began their daily ritual, most had no idea about the political firestorm raging outside their homes. For those of us who waited and waited all night for our new president to emerge, we had gone to bed know the next day would be a historic one.

Many people had turned off their televisions early in the evening thinking Al Gore was on his way to victory.

Many believe some voters on the east coast and in the south, depressed over the apparent Gore victory, did not attempt to go to the polls. America's major television networks had told them it was over so why vote? The role the television news organizations played in the election is an entire issue in itself but it deserves some careful study.

As we all awoke from our slumber, we learned of the pending results and the dramatic events of the previous evening. As I strolled through my office, many had no idea what was happening. A young Democrat who worked with me, Robert Litt, even congratulated me. Both of us were political junkies and had discussed the election at length since we had started working together four months previous.

"Congratulations," he said.

"No way. You didn't hear?" I said.

"Hear what?"

I then went into exhausting detail of the events that unfolded after my young friend had gone to bed. He had seen Bush announced the winner and then went to bed to make sure he was fresh for work the next day.

His sense of disbelief was common amongst most people, Republicans and Democrats, who all assumed the election had come to an end. For most of us, that next day of work took a back seat in many ways to the situation our nation found itself in.

As America's journalists tried to sort out the details from the previous evening, things kept getting more bizarre. Our nation had never seen a presidential candidate retract their concession speech and then vow to fight on. No one. Not even Nixon in 1960. He had reason to but decided against it and ran and won in 1968.

As the details became available, we all were glued once again to our computers and televisions with the blow-by-blow recount of what happened the night before. The most surreal and Hollywood-like story revolved around Gore's concession and later his retraction.

Here is how it all happened:

▶ Between 1:30 a.m. and 1:45 a.m. CST, Gore calls Bush to concede the election. Gore's call comes after the media report that Gore is losing Florida by 50,000 votes and after TV networks call the state — and the election — for Bush.

▶ Gore leaves his hotel in Nashville, Tennessee, and begins the short motorcade drive to War Memorial Plaza, where he will speak to his supporters gathered there.

▶ When the motorcade is about two blocks from the Plaza, field director Michael Whouley pages Gore's traveling chief of staff Michael Feldman. Whouley tells Feldman that Gore trails by just 6,000 votes in Florida, according to the Florida secretary of state, with a thousands of votes still needing to be counted.

▶ Feldman calls Gore campaign chairman William Daley and gives him the latest numbers from Florida. Daley tells Gore how close Florida still is.

▶ When Gore's motorcade reaches War Memorial Plaza, the difference in Florida is fewer than 1,000 votes.

▶ Gore, Daley and other campaign advisers meet in the vice president's holding room at the plaza to discuss the situation and their next move.

▶ About 2:15 a.m. CST: Daley calls Bush campaign chairman Don Evans.

▶ Between 2:30 a.m. and 2:45 a.m. CST, Gore calls Bush again, and the two candidates speak for a few minutes. The conversation's "contents are private," the Gore camp says, but officials tell CNN that Gore retracted his earlier concession.

▶ Gore leaves War Memorial Plaza to return to his hotel. He does not speak to the crowd.

▶ Daley addresses the plaza crowd. "Our campaign continues," he says, until a winner is officially declared in Florida. The few hundred people remaining in the plaza cheer: "Stay and fight!" and "Don't give up!"

▶ Gore meets with staff until 3:45 a.m. CST and then goes to bed.

▶ Bush and President Clinton scrap planned public statements for now.

The movie-script like events from the previous night had everyone holding their breath. The election still was undecided and many Americans could not understand how it could be so close. With voter turnout at all-time lows, the fact the fight for the presidency could be decide by only a few thousand votes was remarkable.

Later in the day, a transcript of Gore's call to Bush was released to the media. Just reading the first few lines, you can imagine the feelings both candidates must have had. It occurred at 2:30 a.m. EST.:

GORE: Governor Bush, circumstances have changed

BUSH: Let me make sure I understand this; You're calling me back to retract your concession?

GORE: Well, you don't have to get snippy about this. We need to wait until the vote count is complete.

BUSH: My brother has assured me that the vote is accurate and that I have won Florida.

GORE: Let me explain something to you; your younger brother is not the ultimate authority on this.

BUSH: You have to do what you have to do Mr. Vice President.

Apparently the call ended as abruptly as it began. Bush was obviously ticked and Gore did not hide his feelings for Bush or his brother's control in Florida. Throughout the election, Jeb Bush had told his brother he would deliver the state to him. With its crown jewel of 25 electoral votes, both candidates needed the state in a close race. It seemed to be a battle from day one of the campaign but many believed the younger Bush would help his brother win the Presidency by carrying the state where he was the sitting governor. No one had any idea just how crucial Florida would be.

What was apparent from the early morning throughout the day was the fact Florida would have to conduct an automatic recount of all its ballots to help certify the winner in the close race. Florida law mandated in close races a machine recount of ballots to ensure the accuracy of the first count. Florida had become America's version of Pandora's Box and the content of that box would bring the nation to the brink of an all out Constitutional crisis.

Early in the morning on November 8th, in an almost orchestrated protest, voters in Palm Beach County were complaining about the county's "butterfly ballot." Many of the voters claimed that had mistakenly voted for Pat Buchanan instead of Gore due to the confusing nature of the ballot. They demanded a revote and were soon joined by a circus of Democratic allies including Jesse Jackson and Alan Dershowitz. Three voters carried their personal battle a step further by filing lawsuits to demand a revote due to their contention that the butterfly ballots were confusing. In Jackson and Dershowitz, they had the clowns in place and the three-ringed circus was ready to begin.

The fact that Jackson and Dershowitz flew to south Florida so quickly should be enough to show how futile such political set-ups can be. Both Jackson and Dershowitz, two of the nation's worst media whores, immediately began charging racism and violations of civil rights because of the ballots. It so happened that a majority of those complaining about the ballots were either black or Jewish. How a ballot could be racist or anti-Semitic is beyond me. If I am correct, a ballot doesn't change its form if your skin is brown or if you celebrate Hanukah.

In this humble American's opinion, the whole ballot protest was little more than a desperate Democratic Party looking for a way to overturn the results of the election. Under the guise of protecting our sacred democracy, these Democrats and their media prostitutes immediately began to make as much noise as possible to deflect what was really happening in Florida. That day I wrote for the *Strategic Jungle Syndicate*:

Palm Beach Ballot Question Ludicrous

The Democrats are a desperate bunch.

I am not a person who gets very angry often but the attempt by the Democratic Party to raise questions about the validity of the presidential race in Florida is almost comical.

The premise of the Democratic argument is that the ballot for president in this heavily Democratic district in Florida was so confusing voters mistakenly voted for Reform candidate Pat Buchanan instead of their man Al Gore.

It may sound harsh but if these people made

that type of error, they deserve to feel bad.
Maybe next time they'll learn from their
mistake. It's time to get over it and learn
how to vote like a responsible American. In
fact, if these voters pay so little attention to
the ballot they are punching, I have serious
doubts about their mental faculties and why
they are voting in the first place.

It's scary to consider these people may have
a driver's license too.

I've looked at the ballot hundreds of times
since yesterday. I honestly tried to
understand how an adult American could
make this mistake. I, myself, find it very
hard to believe that so many people could
have made the mistake that we should hold
another election. The damn arrow lines up
with the corresponding punch card hole.
How can people complain? If the voted paid
so little attention to where they were
punching their ballot, they deserve to lose
their vote.

What takes even more steam out of this
childish argument is both the Republican
and Democratic parties in the area approved
the ballot weeks before the election. The
whiny Democrats had their opportunity to
have the ballot changed and didn't.

The reason they didn't have it changed was
arrogance. How does arrogance play into the
equation? It's simple really. Gore's campaign
advisors went into the election overconfident

in Florida and across the nation. They underestimated George W. Bush from the beginning and now it's coming back to bite them in the backside.

I've heard no mention in the mainstream media about reports that Democratic election officials intimidate voters in Florida, tried to distract poll watchers and even campaigned inside polling places violating Federal law. The liberal media has hid these allegations because they too have a stake in Gore winning the presidency.

There is no question this is a close election. We won't know the end result until later today or perhaps right before Thanksgiving. But the Democrats, in true Clinton-like manner, are simply sore losers who now want to make the nation suffer because of their loss. They are willing to create a Constitutional crisis that could divide our nation further to keep their stranglehold on the White House. That's both selfish and irresponsible.

The circus that is now running in south Florida is an embarrassment that could further alienate more of the populous from the political process. Self-serving, egotistical men like Jesse Jackson have descended on Florida like a vulture over a dying animal. They want face time and another way to make money off a hollow cause.

The Democrats and Al Gore lost and they are

in denial. They lost Tuesday and are about to lose again today. The sad part is they want every American to go down the tubes with them.

Now that's leadership.

Everyone knew it would be a close election. No one had any doubt it may come down to a dogfight over one state. But the fact that Gore appeared to have won the popular vote and Bush the Electoral College was indeed a surprise. Many conservatives had predicted the opposite would happen.

But for the Democrats to parade blacks and other minorities in the streets of south Florida claiming the ballot was unfair, was, well, hysterical. At the same time, the very people they claimed to be defending were degraded further. If it were I, I wouldn't want to be known as the idiot who couldn't figure out a simple ballot punch card.

I can understand some elderly voters having problems. The fact remains we must be held accountable for all our decisions in life. In this day and age of political correctness, no one wants to accept personal responsibility. It's always someone else's fault and here was the incumbent Vice President asking us to believe that a simple paper ballot confused voters.

That didn't fly with me but still the mess in West Palm Beach marched on.

To a certain degree, I think most of America was numb. Not since 1876 had an election been so close and under a cloud of uncertainty. In an America where news was brought to you live as it happened, most Americans expected the instant election result they had become accustomed to. As a 30-something Generation X'er, I had never had to wait for election results.

I can remember the old IBM PC that first crept into my high school classroom in 1986, but I am pretty much a technology driven professional. I admit it freely that I am accustomed to instant gratification with news and information. I grew up with cable television, CNN and live satellite news. Vietnam was the first war to be televised but even then the news was 24-48 hours old. By 1991 and the Persian Gulf War in Iraq, we could watch bombs as they dropped on their target. It reminds me a lot of Slim Pickens riding the ICBM in the classic film "Dr. Strangelove." Except now, war was more antiseptic. Unlike Vietnam, you didn't see the human damage. The government learned from Vietnam and no longer let us view the real damage.

Understanding how dependent we had all become on instant news, 24-hours per day, it's easy to see how people woke on November 8 and were stunned.

Immediately the Democratic machine kicked into high gear. Representative Robert Wexler, a Democrat from Florida, went on television acting as though someone had just disparaged his mother. Wexler charged an additional 19,000 ballots in Palm Beach County had been disqualified due to a faulty ballot. Wexler all but accused some country poll workers of interfering in the vote and Democrats all over the nation went on the offensive.

This was very disconcerting to me as a Republican and an American. Having suffered through the Clinton debacle, I viewed the second day of the election as another assault on our democracy by an unethical and win-at-all-costs group of politicians who had lost and simply did not want to give up the power the enjoyed abusing.

Public opinion polls at the outset proved most Americans liked Clinton and the job he had done over this two terms. Even during his impeachment, Clinton continued to charm. That was a truly scary thing. Whenever a leader can do whatever they want with no repercrsions, everyone should be worried. Did Clinton do anything while he was in office? Sure, there were some small victories I would concede helped the country but for the most part Bill Clinton ruled for Bill Clinton.

It was this decisive feeling amongst Republicans and Democrats that resulted in a such a close election. It was obvious we were a nation completely divided. Divided between what we had been for the past eight years and what many of us wanted to become for the sake of our small children and the crumbling family unit.

But this undecided election was tearing at us again.

As the story continued to unfold on November 8, Hollywood producers and scriptwriters had to be jealous. Suddenly, you had a state's election thrown into turmoil holding up the election of the 43rd President of the United States. Throw on top of that Bush's own brother Jeb Bush was the Governor of the Florida and sat on the state's Election Canvassing Committee and you could see things would only get more difficult.

To handle the confusion in Florida, both candidates sent to Florida former White House cabinet members to oversee the process of recounting the ballots and to protect each candidate's interests in this post-election drama. Vice

President Al Gore sent former Secretary of State Warren Christopher and Bush sent the bulldog James Baker, the former Chief of Staff under his father. Both lent credibility to what was about to begin in Florida.

By anyone's account, both Christopher and Baker were honorable men who would make sure the recount and the ensuing battle for the public's support. But it was Baker's smoothness and cocky drawl that made most Republicans breathe a bit easier knowing someone of his stature would be watching the hen house. While Baker seemed to be heading to Florida to double check Bush's win, it was Christopher's announcement two days later that would start the battle.

EIGHT
Oh, Come On!

November 9

What the hell was going on? Here we were, three full days after the election and still the result was in doubt. The machine recounts were moving forward and breakneck speed in Florida while America waited. The public relations battle had kicked into high gear. Both sides had their party line and both played it pretty well.

The Democrats did what they do so well; they scream, insult and utilize the fear of Americans to get their way. Now, I realize that statement is on its merit partisan, but it is the truth. One thing I have learned in my short life is that when it come to politics, you do what you have to win. Because the Democrats have so little wiggle room with their stilted arguments, they result to personal and vicious attacks.

On the third day of the broken election, the Democrats began their offensive. The mandatory machine recounts were revealing a Bush victory, although the lead Bush once enjoyed in the thousands would be reduced to just a few hundred votes. This obviously interfered with Gore's plans to win the White House and ensure another four years of Democratic rule.

After 25 pages of notes and thoughts written via pen and paper, I have come to the conclusion that the Gore campaign had planned on charging head with a plan should the vice president lose a very close race. Again, reading this book it's no secret that I am a passionate conservative and a Republican. But timing is the key. Hours before the mandatory machine recount was complete, the Democrats and the Gore campaign immediately put the wheels in motion to ask for manual hand recounts in heavily Democratic precincts and counties to "pick up" votes with the chance to change the results of the election. When Warren Christopher strolled to the microphone on the afternoon of the 9th, it was clear the election was far from over.

"We have always believed that every American must have their vote counted. To that end, we are requesting a manual recount in Palm Beach, Dade, Broward and Volusia

Counties. We believe there were significant irregularities in these counties that may have discarded legal votes. Those votes need to be counted."

In a few sentences, Christopher outlined what the Gore campaign would repeat over and over again in their effort to keep counting votes until the results equaled a win for their man. Democrats quickly clawed their way onto the nation's television shows pleading their case making statements that the Republicans. Suddenly, the sore loser was becoming the voice of the disenfranchised voters whose votes were "never counted."

The fact is, all votes were counted through the machine recount. The Democratic stance that votes were thrown out illegally and that the voice of the voters in Florida was not being heard was on its face false. But still, half of America believed it and wouldn't dig deeper through the barrage of liberal media to find the truth.

But still, I believed in the system and pronounced to my coworker on that day "Don't worry, by the end of the day it will be over and George W. Bush will be president."

November 10

It was official – or was it? The mandatory machine recount had been completed and sure enough, Bush had won for a second time. This time, by the skin of his teeth with the official Florida tally now at 327 votes.

That was it. Game over. Gore, go home. Democrats get ready for a new game in town. The Bush presidency would sweep in and save us from ourselves and the decadent 1990s.

But a judge in Palm Beach County stopped the county from certifying its votes. It was now up to three Democratic members of the Palm Beach Canvassing Board to decide whether or not to proceed with a hand recount in the heavily Democratic enclave.

Many on the left will consider this to be some kind of right-wing conspiracy theory but I make no apologies. In my heart of hearts, I know the plan to push for hand recounts was a planned assault by Democratic operatives and the Gore campaign to try and tip the scales in their favor should the election be as close as it was.

Do I have proof? No. But several news reports, primarily from conservative watchdog media like NewsMax.com and World Net Daily reported weeks before the election that such a plan was in place. The key was no one thought they could pull it off let alone to decide the entire election.

Nonetheless, late on the evening of the 10th, the three members of the Palm Beach Canvassing Board voted to conduct a complete manual recount of all 600,000+ ballots in the county after a smaller count of one percent of the ballots had revealed some problems in the tabulation. These problems were nothing new to Palm Beach County or to most polling places across America.

The fact is, each state and each county in the United States has a certain margin of error when the ballots are counted via a computer or the human eye. It's a bi-product of our open election system that sets no national standard on what constitutes a legal vote or what ballots should be used. Despite this general rule of thumb regarding the inaccuracy of many elections, Democratic supporters climbed to their local hilltop and screamed racism, disenfranchisement and anything else that made it look as though G.W. was trying to steal the election.

Think about that for a moment. The man won the election, not once but twice. If you win the initial count, and then a machine recount of every ballot in the state, how can you be stealing the election? The notion that "every vote should be counted" was a romantic one but in reality it never happens. Most Americans had not realized this because no other high-profile national race had ever been so close and our elected officials or the slanted media had never raised attention to the problems with vote tabulation in the United States.

If you talk to people in inner city areas like South Central Los Angeles, the south side of Chicago or in Harlem, they'll tell you about these problems and how far back they stretch. Before it meant a Gore defeat, no one mentioned this. Jesse Jackson wasn't smart enough, or didn't care enough, to push for election reform prior to his friend Gore losing due to these problems. Why is it that the Democratic leaders never have a problem with the playing field unless they've stepped on it and slipped?

Despite this inappropriate use of an issue, the Palm Beach Canvassing Board moved ahead. They set in motion a plan to count the ballots by hand and to consciously miss the state mandated certification date of November 14th in order to recount the ballots.

It was no surprise that Bush felt like he had just been robbed. The Bush team, who had been criticizing the Gore camp for even thinking about going to court of the election results, now found themselves inserting their foot in their mouth as they appealed to the 11th Circuit Court of Appeals in Atlanta, Georgia, on November 12th to halt the manual recounts in Florida. Their contention was the recounts violated Bush's Constitutional rights to due process therefore must be stopped. All agreed the Bush suit was a long shot and more than that, it hurt him in the ever important public relations battle. Since Bush's team had chastised even the chance of Al Gore going to court to challenge the election results in Florida, the fact that Bush and the Republicans were going to court hurt the cause.

Again, Florida Democrat Robert Wexler went on the offensive.

"The Republicans have been crying about the use of the judicial system to decide the outcome of this election yet they are the first ones to file any court papers," Wexler said on CNN. "What are they afraid of is the question the American people should be asking. If Bush is confident he won, he should let the counts proceed."

His comments made sense to most Americans. Why wouldn't Bush want the recounts to reaffirm his victory? Why wouldn't he want his legitimacy to be supported but winning yet another vote count?

The answer is simple. Bush, and many of us, realized the Democratic intent was not to find the true intent of the voter. The Democrats, who had used similar tactics over the past 20 years to help elect local officials, knew the ensuing chaos and doubt caused by the labor-intensive manual recount would help them overturn the results of the election and catapult Gore to the presidency. You didn't read that in your local newspaper or hear the talking heads on CNN report on it. Obviously the specter of having a conservative in the White House did not thrill the liberal media establishment. Again, the media bias raises its head. I'll discuss that in length during another chapter.

During the waning hours of November 12th, the number of lawsuits claiming votes were not counted or absentee ballots were cast illegal climb further clouding the picture on who will be the next president.

As for me, I sat glued to my television and computer waiting for the next dip on the roller coaster ride that seemed to last forever.

NINE

Ladies and Gentlemen · Katherine Harris

November 13

Finally, the Republican world woke to some good news. The Florida Secretary of State, Katherine Harris, stated she would not extend the deadline of November 14th at 5 p.m. to allow for the hand recounts in Palm Beach County and now Dade County to be completed. Under Florida law, according to Harris' interpretation, all vote totals had to be forwarded to her office for official certification by the end of day to make Florida's votes official and send them to the national archive in Washington for Electoral College purposes.

Harris, the attractive and seemingly patriotic Secretary of State, immediately became the target of Democratic hate mongers. Her association with the Bush campaign instantly subjected her ethical judgment to the highest critique from blatant Democratic sympathizers like CBS' Dan Rather and the entire CNN clan.

Harris had served as the Bush campaign's chairperson in Florida and Harris had even spent time on the campaign trail with Bush. At first, this sounded explosive to the media but in reality it was little more than a smokescreen. Harris had been elected by popular vote, meaning Democrats and Republicans voted her in, and her political affiliation was not an issue. The Gore camp immediately blasted Harris' decision and promised to take her to court to try and force her to accept the amended results to include the hand recounts.

One key Gore campaign spokesperson referred to Harris as a "commissar like those in the former Soviet Union." They vilified this Harvard graduate and plotted ways to expose her to public scrutiny.

But still, Harris stuck to her guns and listened to her state legal counsel informing her she was doing what was necessary under Florida law.

Within 10 minutes of Harris' press conference, Gore campaign chief William Daley, son of the infamous Mayor Richard Daley of Chicago, stood before the media and promised a legal challenge of Harris' decision not to accept vote totals after the state-mandated time of 5 p.m. on November 14.

"We want to reiterate our position that every vote should be counted. It is the basis of our democracy – one man, one vote," Daley said. "The Secretary of State has chosen to ignore those votes and we feel she is making a decision based on politics instead of state law."

And so, it began. The son of the most infamous vote stealing scheme in American history started the real court battles that would stretch on. Daley's father had stolen the election for Kennedy in 1960 and now his son was trying to accomplish the feat for vice president Al Gore.

The day ended on a negative note as the 11th Circuit Court denied Bush's request to stop the hand recounts in Florida. I was livid. For all that Al Gore had cried that "every vote should be counted," he was now telling me my voted didn't count. The court victory for Gore slammed me back to reality. A reality that I felt was about to shock my senses and force me to give up on the system I felt I was fighting so hard to save.

November 14

Because of Harris' order to the various Florida counties concerning vote certification, Palm Beach voted to stop counting its ballots as it petitioned to the Supreme Court of Florida to require Harris to give them more time to complete the count. As Palm Beach stopped, Dade County began its selected manual recount of handpicked Democratic precincts to decide if it would go on with a complete recount of all precincts. The tide seemed to be going the Bush way but the ups-and-downs of the last week were wearing on America.

On a personal level, I had been engulfed by the election drama. My whole world seemed upside down. Eliete and I were expecting our second child, a boy, and he was now a week overdue. That meant that the 15th would be the day the doctor induced labor.

Throughout the day, walking around work and in between listening to CNN on my computer, I told people my son wouldn't arrive until the time was right.

"He's waiting until we have a Republican president," I joked with my coworkers.

I believed, at that point, that he would be born with George W. Bush as the President-elect. Harris had set the deadline and once that deadline had passed, it was over. Right?

Wrong.

Due to enormous political pressure, and the demonstrations orchrastrated by the left, Harris agreed to extend the deadline by one day. She required each of the three heavily Democratic counties to submit, in writing, by 2 p.m. on November 15th their reasoning why they needed an extension. Florida law had allowed for an extension of the deadline at the discretion of the Secretary of State. Harris would review these written explanations from the canvassing boards and decide whether or not to extend the deadline further. If the reasons were not sufficient, Harris would certify the election results at 5 p.m. on November 15 seemingly putting an end to the weeklong election fiasco.

So there it was. By the end of my son's first day on earth, G.W. would be president. It appeared to be the end game. How would the Democrats get around Florida law? They hadn't counted on Harris and the discretion of the Secretary of State and now it spelled doom for their man Gore.

I was pretty cocky about it. I called my Democratic buddies and congratulated them on a good fight but told them it was over. I was pretty sure. Surely nothing else could happen to change the course of the election again, right?

In discussions around the office, conversation turned towards Gore's chances in 2004. As throughout the drama, I had my morning talk with my younger coworker Robert Litt.

"Rob, if he concedes now, he looks like a helluva guy and he'll win by a landslide in 2004," I said. "The next four years he can lead the charge for election reform and the guy will be golden."

"You're right. He's got to concede. I hate to say that but he's got to quit. We'll see. They're still counting votes," Robert said.

They were still counting but it seemed ridiculous. Still, there were good points on the other side. In one of his emails on the subject to me, the young Mr. Litt wrote this that made good sense:

——Original Message——
From: Robert Litt
Sent: Thursday, November 14, 2000 11:24 AM
To: Scott Gulbransen
Subject: Question

Here is my question for you: If Bush truly wanted a clean election and an un-tainted victory why wouldn't he just let the hand-count to happen? He already has his cabinet in place and time isn't an issue. If a hand count assures accuracy than why would he object? A hand count will assure the American people, who are being played like fools, a true count. Now, Bush can't object to a hand count with a straight face because back in 1996 he suggested a hand count in a Texas congressional race. Your thoughts...

At first glance, my younger friend made some strong points. Sitting there at my desk on November 12th I thought long and hard about what my answer was. Why not count the votes by hand to make sure the will of the people was heard? I know if it was me running for office, and my victory hinged on an accurate count of votes, I would want a count to make sure it's right. After all, could it be us information junkies just wanted a quick resolution because we were used to it? My answer to my friend was this:

——Original Message——
From: Scott Gulbransen
Sent: Thursday, November 14, 2000 11:27 AM
 To: Robert Litt
 Subject: RE: Question

 In two words: human error.

Rob, in all reality, if you have a bunch of democrats who are counting votes by hand, and determining the intention of voters, that's dangerous. While your question is a good one on the surface, dig deeper and you can imagine. Imagine if it was the other way. Would you trust a bunch of 60-year old Republicans counting ballots if their guy needed a few hinder more to win? Do I think they would cheat on purpose, probably not. But that's why they use machines. It takes bias and emotion out of the equation and is fair.

You'll notice I shot the email back in just three minutes. That's how tied in I was to this thing. I lived, breathed, ate, slept and talked the election. My response may seem like the company line but let me expand on my thoughts at the time.

The whole premise that the initial count was not accurate and that Bush may be winning even though he didn't receive the majority of the votes had no basis. The Democrats charging this never once delivered any evidence that such an inaccurate count occurred. In fact, Democrats and the left-brained media promised recounts even after the election was decided. They said they would use Florida's "Sunshine Law," the state equivalent of the Freedom of Information Act, to count the votes even if judges deemed it illegal or not required. The Democrats would, in a worst-case scenario in their political book of dirty tricks, try to drag through the mud G.W. if it was the last action before they sucked in their final breath. This type of attitude is what turned me off from the Democratic Party to begin with.

But the core of Robert's message, although he has a good head on his shoulders and I consider him a good friend, was flawed, in my opinion. Why wouldn't Bush want another count to reaffirm his victory?

Easy, he knew he was about to be screwed. Imagine taking your Scholastic Aptitude Test and, after passing it, you're asked to take it again to "just make sure you really passed it." Or, after winning the lottery, state officials turn to you and say, "We're going to re-draw the numbers to make sure your six numbers come up again and indeed you win this $80 million."

My Democratic friends continued on with their fight. Kevin Wynn, who had worked at a Las Vegas public relations firm with me, also thought along the same lines as Robert. He, in his true Massachusetts political way, demanded "all the votes be counted." The premise he followed was the same of Democratic leaders of congress who were littering my television with their leftist babble. Here was Kevin's email to me on the that day:

——Original Message——
From: Kevin Wynn
Sent: Thursday, November 14, 2000 1:33 AM
 To: Scott Gulbransen
 Subject: RE: It's Over!

It will not be over, and should be, until all the votes are counted. How can we disenfranchise thousands of voters and, in turn, perhaps disenfranchise millions of others.

Scott, voting is the root of our democracy and how can we possibly have a president elected without counting the votes. That would be a sad day for us all.

I know we'll never agree on this but I know you agree that every person's vote must be accounted for.

I'm proud to call Kevin my friend but, again, the idea that votes were not counted is unproven today as it was on November 14, 2000. Kevin is a patriot at heart and a highly intelligent man whom things through his politics. He doesn't pick up the New York Times and say "Yeah, that sounds good." He formulates his own opinions based on the vast amounts of reading he does. So I respected his opinions and always listened. I never, ever, have taken his, or any of my Democratic friends' political disagreements with me as personal. To make politics personal is unjust to you and the person you disagree with.

Just as I too am a product of my environment, so is Kevin. Born and raised in a suburb of Boston, Kevin was a true-blue Democrat – always has been, always will be. I respect that and applaud his strong sense of patriotism and the desire to stick by those who mostly follow his personal beliefs.

I also need to say; he is wrong.

He'll love that line.

Early in the day, Florida Circuit Judge Terry Lewis orders the recounts to stop. His decision, even though he personally was a Democrat, was the accurate decision based on Florida law and the right of the secretary of state to certify the results of the election of Florida at the set date and time.

To me, it was a forgone conclusion that Harris would deny any request by the three counties to accept results after the 5 p.m. deadline on November 15. But because of the Democratic threats and character assassination that had already occurred once Harris became involved, she had no choice but to at least consider the late totals.

But was anyone really fooled? In my mind, it was clear that Florida law required Harris to declare the results of the election by the deadline that had been set forth by the Florida Legislature. I had a real difficult time understanding what the other side was trying to do. The Democrats kept screaming that the election was being stolen yet they themselves seemed to want to put aside all the laws that would prevent anyone from stealing an election.

To try and make light of a very disturbing situation, my column on the Strategic Jungle Syndicate reflected my smart-ass mood:

As the Florida recount debacle hopefully comes to an end, you can't help but want to just get the whole thing over with. As a staunch Bush supporter, I found myself actually thinking I didn't care who won as long as we put an end to the madness. If that person was Al Gore, so be it. If it was Bush, I would be much happier knowing my new son would enter the world under a new Republican president. The argument we have heard over the past week from the Gore campaign has been the have an interest in ensuring no voters are alienated and that the will of the voters is heard. When listening to this liberal spin, I found myself thinking about the hit television show "Survivor". Although I never watched the show (despite my wife's keen interest in if "gay" Rich would win), I felt like a contestant this past week. As you may know, the show plunks down a bunch of egotistical moneygrubbers on a tropical island who then have an opportunity to gang up on each other and vote people off at the conclusion of each broadcast. I felt this too compelling to think of how things would have gone if we had selected our next president that way.

If I was in charge of the 2000 Presidential Election version of "Survivor", here is a list of the inhabitants and whom I would vote off the island and the reasons why.

Election Survivor 2000 Contestants: Vice President Al Gore, President-elect - er-Texas Governor George W. Bush, the Rev. Jesse Jackson, Florida Governor Jeb Bush, Palm Beach County Commissioner Carol Roberts, Gore Campaign Chairman Bill Daley, Florida Secretary of State Katherine Harris and me!

1. First Vote - Jesse Jackson. Jesse Jackson is perhaps the best example of what happens when a man becomes so enamored with seeing his mug on television he'll do anything to get it there. Jackson rushes to the sight of any controversy to garner face time and throw the race card into the mix. There's no question the African-American population needs a vocal and visible leader. But a man that can barely speak in clear English should not be it. Jesse cares about Jesse and the sooner people realize that, the better. Bye Jesse - you've been kicked out of MY island.

2. Second Vote - Jeb Bush. Et tu Jeb? How could you let your brother down? Florida should not have been this close. So I give you the boot and at least send you with a lifejacket and some food
- you are a Republican.

3. Third Vote - Carol Roberts. This Palm Beach County Commissioner reminds me of the wide-eyed slot machine junkies I used to see in Las Vegas. Her nasty demeanor and partisan politics have here swimming off my island. She does swim with sharks (see AL GORE) to begin with so don't worry she'll be fine.

4. Fourth Vote - Bill Daley. It's like 1960 all over again. Like father, like son. Getting Daley off the island would be tough with all those labor union guys ready to break my legs. Hope I don't end up in the end zone at Giants Stadium like Hoffa. Once Daley leaves the island, suddenly the stench goes away.

5. Fifth Vote - Al Gore. Let's face it; he's too boring. You can only take so much of a man that has no rhythm or personality. Plus, with Tipper waiting at home, he kept shutting off our boom box playing the incomparable Kid Rock. Of course it would take over a week to get him off

the island. I can see it now; "We have to make sure
someone put out my flame and to ensure those who
wanted to keep my flame lit are heard. This is about the
will of the Survivors." Uh, no. Bye Al. Just as we banished
him, a helicopter full of Buddhist monks swooped down
and offered to take him back to Washington.

6. Sixth Vote · Katherine Harris. This was a tough one.
As Dubya and I sat on the beach, it was hard to vote the
captivating Harris off the island. An intelligent Harvard
graduate with looks to match the wits, had to be voted off
and we extinguished her flame. But being that we are
both married, and able to control our urges, unlike a soon-
to-be ex-President from Arkansas · oh, New York, we said
goodbye. We gave her a hero's goodbye for fighting for
justice.

7. Seventh Vote · Me. What? Did you think I would vote
off the next president of the United States? Unlike Al
Gore, I can be a statesman and step aside for the true
winner to step forward and lead. As I shake Dubya's
hand, he smiles and tells me he's been reading me on the
Strategic Jungle Syndicate for a long time. "Nice work on
that border shooting. I'll have Secretary McCain look into
it." With that, I climb on my inflatable elephant and start
paddling for shore.

Just as it should have been on Election Day, Bush won.

This bit of comic relief seemed to fit in with the
present atmosphere. Gore must now accept the ruling of
the courts in Florida today and move forward. It's time to
fall on your sword Al, even though you should have done
it a week ago.

This is all about winning and losing. The Democrats, used to the Clinton lies and underdog victories, cannot face the fact that they lost. And if they are not careful, they may wish to be sent to a deserted island to hide from the will of Americans who know better.

Of course Al Gore and his fellow Democratic machine immediately appealed the decision to the Florida Supreme Court. Most media outlets described the court as an "activist" court made up of all but one Democratic appointees. That didn't bode well for Bush and the rest of us Republicans looking for an end to the madness.

November 15

The eighth day of the broken election was somewhat quiet for the public. On this day, all of the political moving would be done in the law offices of lawyers for both sides. Those legal moves being planned behind closed doors would become the stuff movies are made of. I'm sure no less than 10 or so attorneys will write their books highlighting how they outsmarted the other guy.

The day began with anticipation as the country waited for Harris' decision on the recounts and whether she would extend the deadlines for Palm Beach, Miami-Dade and Valousa Counties to complete the arduous task of counting the ballots by hand. There was a sense Republicans, with the election results residing in the conservative hands of Harris, had finally overcome Gore's challenges and were on the brink of capturing the White House for the firs time since 1988.

At the same time the nation waited, Broward County decided to start their own recount. A partial count had revealed some gains for Gore and the county decided to get into the action and begin discerning the intent of the voters themselves. This included ballots that were discarded due to no vote or multiple votes for president. This was preposterous to most Americans because everyone had the sense that the system was flawed and each state had a percentage of votes that were tossed out. Apparently, not all Americans even knew how to vote. I try to have faith in my fellow Americans but if you screw up a ballot, you have issues that go far beyond anything a poll worker could help you with.

In Tallahassee, Katherine Harris smelled something that wasn't quite kosher. The canvassing boards in various counties continued to count despite the law telling them they must certify their votes by 5 p.m. Since these backward thinking canvassing boards decided to ignore Florida law and keep counting and raising doubts about the legitimacy of a Bush presidency, Harris petitioned the Florida Supreme Court to halt the manual recounts and end the drama that had held the nation hostage for over a week.

Harris made a wise move in petitioning the high court in Florida to not only affirm her authority under Florida law, but to also consolidate the multiple lawsuits in the state that threatened to derail the Electoral College process and perhaps make it impossible for Florida to have its voice heard on December 18 when the real election took place around the nation.

For all the good that Harris did, asking for the help of the Florida Supreme Court would come back to haunt her, Bush and the nation.

During this legal wrangling, the political and public relations battle wore on. The Democrats, to their credit, never stopped. They preached from the hilltops and threw in everything from the race card to calls of election fraud to try and intimidate the country into believing the votes had not been counted.

At the risk of sounding like an elitist, I cannot fathom how people, millions of them mind you, were fooled by these empty accusations and pointless legal strategies. Elie and I could not believe our eyes and ears. Dinnertime now became our family hour to watch Fox News Channel and discuss the day's events. But on this day, we had more important things than the legal fight in Florida or who would eventually win out and become president.

9:08 a.m. PST

Ryan Paul Gulbransen, my second child and first son, was born at 9:08 a.m. at Scripps Memorial Hospital in La Jolla, California. For one day, the election didn't matter and the joys of parenthood and my commitment to raising my family and being a loving father were on my mind. As I watched my son come into this world, I wondered what it held in store. Would I raise him well enough so he knew right from wrong? Would he be able to look back on the day he was born and understand what it was all about?

As we celebrate Ryan's birth, I looked toward my daughter Alexis. She was now 3 years old and becoming a spark plug. I tortured myself thinking about what my two children might have to endure in the years to come. The decaying moral structure of our society and realizing, at some point, they would have to study how a president received a blowjob from an intern during the first few years she was alive. What was our nation becoming and what would become of my children's America?

After my wife was released from labor and delivery, it was off to her private room for recovery. Joining us was Alberto, my father-in-law, my mother Cassandra and Alexis. My wife, immediately flipped on the television to see what was going down in the election saga. Now, I had promised myself I wouldn't pay any attention to what was happening in Florida. It was my son's day and nothing would distract me from what was important.

Then, sitting their inside the hospital room next to my wife and new son, the word came down. It was still dragging on. No concession speech from Gore and no legal resolution.

"They're all Democrats, are you surprised," Elie said.

"I guess not. But I had faith in the judicial system."

"I'm telling you Scott, the U.S. Supreme Court is going to decide this thing. Mark my words," Elie said.

Now, my wife and I always joke with one another on how each thinks the other always believes they are right. This time, my wife was dead on. I believed the election would be resolved quickly because I had faith in two things that let me down: one was the judicial system and the other was the American people. I never thought the courts would be so biased and the American people, at least half of them, blind. But that was where we were. Half of the population was buying it and that scared the patriot in me.

There's no doubt that Adolf Hitler was a murderous crazy man. The reason I bring up his name at this juncture is understanding how Germany could have believed his lies and followed such a diabolical maniac. After watching what many Americans did and said during the 2000 election, it's makes more sense to me now.

Many people, who were uneducated about the process and the facts, were easy for certain interest groups to sway and have them believe there was something happening in Florida that was in effect stealing a victory from Al Gore. People didn't understand the Electoral College, the U.S. Constitution and other basic related to how we select our presidents. When I say "educated" I'm not meaning to say someone who didn't go to college wouldn't understand and was eager to succumb to their blindness and follow whomever seemed righteous.

As the evening closed, the election was still unresolved and I prayed to God that something would happen and that he would save us from ourselves. I watched little Ryan sleep and looked out the window at the crisp southern California sky. What would happen next, I wondered.

TEN
The Court Jesters

November 17

As difficult as it is to admit this, on the morning of the 17th, I shared the view of many Democrats. I just wanted the election over. If that meant Al Gore as our President, then so be it. I could move to Italy and support my family however I could. Seriously, I wanted it over.

Come on America, someone step up, be a man and concede. As divisive as Richard Nixon was on the political landscape of America, he had the sense to concede in 1960 despite May Richard Daley's hijacking of votes in Chicago that carried Jack Kennedy to the White House.

Why couldn't Gore just concede and come back in four years and try again. It was the American way. If you don't succeed, try again. America loves the loser in so many ways.

We, more than any other country on earth, love to give people a second chance. America was built on a second chance.

The country was again the victim of the waiting game. Bush had filed a motion with the Federal court in Atlanta again trying to stop the manual recounts while Gore filed to the same court saying Bush had no right to try and stop the counts.

7 a.m. PST

Florida Circuit court judge Terry Lewis was ready to decide on the Gore campaign's request. The announcement, read by court clerk Terry Casse, had me sitting on the edge of my seat. Would Lewis rule with his Democratic heart and require Harris to extend her deadline? Or would he do what he was appointed to do – interrupt and uphold the law of Florida?

It was time for the roller coaster to go back up a hill, and tease us Republicans. Lewis ruled for Harris and said she had "exercised her reasoned judgment."

I cheered out load when I watched the reading of the decision on Fox News Channel. Everyone, despite the up and down nature of the post-election fight, had a sense it might finally come to an end. The weeklong battle over votes, under votes, recounts and crooked local canvassing boards all seemed to be over. Katherine Harris now had the trump card known, to most of us regular non-power hungry Americans, as the law. Harris now had the ability to certify the Florida vote and give the presidency to Bush. But of course, it would not be that simple.

Moments after Lewis' judgment upholding standing Florida law, Gore's campaign chief William Daley immediately appealed the decision to the Florida Supreme Court.

Daley and the Gore campaign didn't look upset or worried. In fact, in announcing their plan to appeal after what could have been a gut-wrenching loss in court, the campaign smiled. They smiled as if they knew there was nothing to worry about. At the time, I thought it was just denial.

"How can Daley sit there and look like they just went for a nice dinner," I said to Eliete. "It's over and they stand around like it's nothing big. I don't get it. They're frickin' annoying. It's like Clinton all over again. Comeback Kid – the sequel."

"It's not over yet," Eliete said. "I heard that the Florida Supreme Court is all Democrats. I'm telling you, they're going to screw Bush."

Again, as much as I love my wife and respect her intelligence, I shrugged off her suggestion. State Supreme Court justices are bound by the law, not political points of view. I had every ounce of faith in the *system* that they would make the right decision and put an end to the nightmare.

6 p.m. PST

Watching the various news programs that evening, one message was ringing clear on every channel from every experts mouth: the Florida Supreme Court was no sure thing for G.W. In fact, the court had been known for its "activist" make-up and had proven a propensity to legislate from the bench. Surely in a case that had every eye in America watching their every move, the justices would just follow current law and do what should have been done almost two weeks earlier.

Many billed it as "Gore's last stand." By now, those of us following every development had the sense that Gore would fight on until every single avenue of protest was exhausted. As selfish as it may have been, Gore would not give up. He wasn't concerned with America's pain, he was concerned with holding onto the golden ring of power he had known since his days as a child of a powerful senator growing up in the Watergate Hotel.

Again, I played the optimist. I was confident but careful in my discussions.

"I really think it's over now, Elie. They know that if they rule for Gore it will create a national crisis. They'll follow the law and by Monday Bush will be president."

My wife didn't respond this time. Instead, she gave me the pat and rub on the shoulder she usually gave me when she knew I believed something I was saying but she didn't. She was supporting my wishful thinking and I was doing my best to fool myself.

November 18

It was a glorious Saturday morning in San Diego. The sun was shining and the near 70-degree temperatures flowing through my window made me forget about the madness for a while.

I turned to my left to see my sleeping daughter, who had made a habit of climbing in our bed in the early morning hours, and my wife. I didn't want to wake them but I needed to know what was going on. I couldn't escape this election. So much was riding on it and being three hours behind

Florida, there probably had been activity and I couldn't be in the dark.

I raced down the stairs, past the slumbering dog, into the family room to flip on the television.

I freely admit that I am a news junkie; always have been, always will.

As it flickered to life, I sipped my coffee and waited for some news. The television didn't disappoint me as the news ticked across the screen: "Bush lead extends to 930 after overseas ballots counted."

"Yes," I cheered to an audience of none.

The pundits talked. I listened in my underwear.

Nothing earth shattering this morning - just good news for us Bush Backers. The lead was now almost 1,000. That was big news considering some media reports had the lead down to 100+ votes after partial recounts had been done.

"Give it up Gore. It's over," again, talking to myself.

The election had so become a part of my daily life, I would discuss it at length with myself. Sometimes wondering if my wife would have me committed. Elie was always willing to discuss it with me and she, despite our newborn spending just his second night at home, was beginning to get hooked too. She also started to realize the importance of a Bush win. We were parents now and things change when your parents. You want your kids to have the best but you also don't want them exposed to some of the filth out there.

In our discussions about the issues of the election, Eliete and I agreed on most things. We were both brought up Catholic and in a home with both parents. We wanted to raise our kids with high moral integrity while and the same time teaching them to be compassionate to their fellow human beings. Eliete, being the children of Cuban immigrants, and me, being third-generation immigrants from Russian and Italian grandparents, both love America and consider us patriotic.

We both have close gay friends, friends of all ethnic backgrounds and friends with varying religious and political beliefs. But for us, the recent acceptance of almost every way of life, no matter how disturbing, was wearing on us and we correlated the Clinton-Gore years with that downfall. America had become a nation of whiny, ultra-sensitive fringe groups bent on making the rest of us live by their rules. The traditional family was considered "exclusionary" and to speak of moral or ethical values was tantamount to discrimination.

On the morning of the 18th, these thoughts were racing through my mind. It wasn't my battle I felt I was fighting. It was a battle for my children and for my grandchildren. I wanted morals without discrimination; values that are based on what the majority feels.

If I am a traditional political author, at this point I'd throw a bunch of validating opinions at you via research. But that's not what this is about. This is how I feel and why I feel the way I do. This is the way I felt on November 18th, 2000, and this is how I feel now.

Luckily, it was a relatively slow news day so I could devote my time to my family. We did a little Christmas shopping and had fun on one of our typical family outings. Driving to the mall, I looked back at Alexis to be greeted by her brown eyes and a smile that could melt Superman. Things were good; I was hoping they would get better.

November 19

The Sunday political shows. Lieberman preaching the Gore gospel and Dole preaching my views. Ho, hum. When would it end?

I attended church services at St. Patrick's. I prayed for a quick resolution and even wrote in George W. Bush's name into the community prayer book. It looked like I was the 50th person to do so. That was a good sign.

After also writing in the name of Elvis Presley, something I do each Sunday at church, I prayed a Rosary for G.W. and looked to the heavens for help.

Monday would be a big day as the Supreme Court would hear arguments on why amended election results, those including hand recounts, should be included in the state's certified results. As I climbed into bed that night, I again turned to prayer. I just knew we were on the verge of a breakthrough. I could feel it in the pit you find in your stomach.

November 20

Argument day. Would the will of the people prevail? Or would the strong minority overcome the senses of the Florida Supreme Court?

I made the rounds in the bedroom, kissing my wife, Alexis and Ryan and out the door to work. An avid sports fan and a regular listener to the best all-sports station in America, XTRA-AM 690 in San Diego, on this day, my radio was fixed to news radio. The arguments were underway and I was looking for the latest news tidbit before getting too engulfed in work.

Nothing. Talking heads rehashing the Florida Supreme Court background and the issues before them. I flipped to other news stations: KNX in Los Angeles, KABC, and nothing new.

Work was slow. I was working at a dynamic and stellar public relations and advertising agency that just hadn't given me a ton of work. As much as I like to brag about my strong work ethic, I was glad to have the time to follow what was happening in Florida. As the rest of the staff worked hard and busily moved around the office, I sat glued listening to audio relays of CNN and MSNBC waiting for news. It was 10 a.m. and the arguments were underway. As much as I sat on the edge of my seat, I knew it would be at least 24 hours until the court would make a decision.

The issue for the court: should the amended totals be included in the certified state results. Harris had already said no, using her discretion under Florida law, and now the Democrats were challenging that. They said she had no right and was misinterpreting the law. It was the "woe is me" cry over and over again. Sitting there, I tried to think like the other side and I couldn't. In order for their accusations to be true, it would have to be the largest conspiracy and disregard of the law in American history. It was ludicrous but the liberal media charged on, propping their boy Gore up as the poster child of the U.S. Constitution.

As both sides argued in front of Florida's highest court, the swirling winds of discontent continued to whirl outside. In what would be a severe tactical error for the Gore campaign, a few days earlier the campaign had challenged the legitimacy of almost 2,000 overseas military ballots saying they didn't have postmarks and that they should be thrown out. This strategy immediately backfired as veterans all over the nation protested the Democrats attempt to invalidate the ballots of men and women putting their lives on the line to protect our freedom.

Former Senator Bob Dole, the Republican candidate for president four years earlier in 1996, became the party's spokesperson on the issue directing sharp criticism at Gore and the Democratic Party. Dole, a strong figure in the party, spoke eloquently and proved to be an asset to Bush.

This, to me, was the ultimate in hypocrisy as it relates to Gore and the Democrats' cry during the Florida recount and legal process. Over and over again, Gore and his people continually challenged Bush saying "all the votes must be counted." There was talk of each American's right to vote and how it was being violated because ballots in various Florida counties were not being counted.

Then, suddenly, when they were getting the recounts they wanted and the race was tightening, it was fine to throw out votes and not count them. After all, they were heavily Republican. Gore's people stood in front of me and every other American and lied. What they should have been saying, had they been truthful, was "count the votes as long they are for Al Gore." This ultimate case of sticking your foot in your mouth was quickly addressed on the surface when late in the day, the Democratic Attorney General of Florida, a staunch Gore supporter, urged each county to count the military ballots even if the postmark was missing. Too late, the damage had been done.

The discussion at home turned to how Americans could still believe what was happening in Florida was anything less than the Democrats trying to steal the election.

"Elie? I don't understand how people can sit there and agree with Gore that all votes, even if they were cast incorrectly, should be counted but now want these military votes thrown out. What the hell is going on?"

"Scott, they don't care," Eliete said. "They're looking for anyway to make up the votes so Gore will win. Imagine if they tried to invalidate the votes of another group of people, like Hispanics or Blacks. The Democrats would protest in the streets. It's such hypocrisy."

Ah, now I know why I married her. Smart gal.

The night closed with news that Gore had gained 168 votes in the recounts. Surprise, surprise. Why was it that all the votes that weren't counted the first time were going for Gore? Maybe because they were cheating? I know I'm not crazy and I think logically. The Gore election-stealing machine survived another day and was plotting behind the scenes for even more fireworks.

ELEVEN

Law? What Law?

November 21

When I was a kid, I hated the Heinz 57 ketchup commercial that showed a little boy holding the bottle waiting for the thick ketchup to pour onto his hamburger. As the song "Anticipation" played in the background, my little body grew impatient. I was young and on the run.

"Get on with it kid," I'd yell at the TV.

I'm sure you can understand. I wanted "Speed Racer" to come back on. Speed, Trixy and Racer X had business to take care of and no kid with a slow bottle of ketchup should get in the way.

I was reminded of those feelings again on Tuesday, November 21. The Supreme Court of Florida was weighing the argument of the day before and I wanted it to be over. I kept telling myself they wouldn't dare overturn the decision of Harris and trample of Florida law. I was nervous at work but I just knew this would come to an end. I was 60 percent sure Bush would win this battle and it would be over.

As I read 10 newspapers and around 20 online publications, most had no idea where the court would go. Most were cautiously stating Bush had the upper hand. The Florida law may have been a bit vague but the powers of the Secretary of State were clear – she acted correctly and the vote should be certified minus any of the frivolous recounts that continued throughout the state.

"So, what do you think is going to happen," Robert Litt asked me that day at work.

"Who knows Rob," I said. It seems pretty clear but nothing has been easy during this election."

"Well, if he (Gore) doesn't win, he should concede."

"Rob, you're right but there's no way he will. He can still contest the election and I bet he will."

We both went back to work thinking about what would happen. Rob may have been a staunch Democrat, but he was mature enough to take emotion out of the equation and have a good discussion with a Republican like myself. I wondered why most Democrats couldn't be like Rob. Here was a young kid (22 years old) who was acting much more mature than half the Democratic congressmen and senators appearing on the nation's airwaves. He was passionate about his views but he also realized to be emotional and scream about it doesn't get you anywhere.

5 p.m. PST

Arriving home to one of my wife's patented chicken dinners, we all watched the news for word from the Florida Supreme Court. The news reporters and anchors all joked about the court deciding soon so they could all enjoy their Thanksgiving holiday which was just two days away. Even the spokesperson from the court had come out during the day for an update and talked about making Thanksgiving Day dinner at his aunt's house in Alabama.

"What's taking so long? They're going to extend the deadline," I said.

My father, eating dinner with us that night, pleaded the company line.

"Nah. They won't do it. Bush will win," he said.

"I don't know. They're all Democrats Dad. They're trying to steal this election," I said.

As dinner wrapped up and I moved to the sofa to hold my new son and wind down from the day, I shook my head grew tense. I had a nervous feeling in my stomach and was shaking my foot. I couldn't stop moving and my nervousness was evident. I remember feeling guilty because my mind was so engaged with what was happening, I didn't feel connected to my family. I felt as though I was on an island and waiting for a boat to come rescue me – the U.S.S. G.W. Bush.

Next it was up the stairs to the bedroom to get into something more comfortable. Gray sweatpants and my Krispy Kreme Doughnuts T-shirt. I sat back on our queen-size bed and flipped on Fox News Channel. My wife and kids were now in the room and we just watched.

Then came the bulletin.

6:45 p.m. PST

The Florida Supreme Court had come to a decision and it was time to announce to the nation what their finding was. I quickly made the sign of the cross across my chest and braced for the news.

Time seemed to stand still. I looked at my wife, Alexis and Ryan and watched their faces. My heart beat faster and faster. I could feel my sweat beading off my brow.

"The court hereby orders that the recounts continued and amended results be delivered to the Secretary of State's office no later than 5 p.m. on Sunday, November 26 or 9 a.m. Monday, November 27 if the office is not open on Sunday," the court clerk read from the legal finding.

"No!" Eliete screamed.

"I can't believe it. They're going to steal this election. It's over. They'll find the votes for Gore now," I said with a lump in my throat.

I was so dejected that I laid in bed the rest of the night and just zoned out watching news accounts of what had just happened. The Florida Supreme Court, stunned the conservatives of America and held true to their reputation of being an activist court.

In his post-decision press conference, the cool customer and former Secretary of State James Baker, said it best.

"The Florida Supreme Court has invented a new system for counting election results," Baker said.

Besides doing his job, you could tell Baker was angry. Angry as a Bush agent and angry as an American. I could relate.

Their legislation from the bench made me sick and when you're sick, nothing is better than sleep.

November 22

Strange day.

The day after the legal abomination.

It was also the day before Thanksgiving. It was slow around the office again with many people eating up an extra vacation day to make it a five-day weekend. I sat, as I did for the previous week, glued to my computer screen pondering the next move.

As I surfed from website to website, the headline screamed at me: "Cheney Hospitalized with Chest Pain."

What? Had the election madness finally taken its first victim?

Cheney, who had a history of heart problems, had self-admitted himself to Georgetown Medical Center in Washington. Bush campaign spokesperson Karen Hughes quickly dispelled rumors of a heart attack and said Cheney was alright and would be held for observation due to some chest pain.

It was certainly easy to understand why he would be suffering chest pain. He was perhaps about to become a victim of theft at the hands of the Gore clan. But his seemingly shaky health was an issue that may have reaffirmed some American's opinions that Cheney may not be healthy enough to serve. During the campaign, Democrats had raised the issue of Cheney's health but the Bush people did a nice job of diffusing the issue and it soon went away.

I remember thinking thoughts of anger. Gore and his zealots were now making a man ill with their dirty deeds. Was the power Gore thirsted after so great that he was willing to literally destroy one of his opponents? I know, a little strong but that's the emotion I felt at the time.

By mid-afternoon Bush held a press conference to further squash rumors of a heart attack.

"I just got off the phone with Secretary Cheney and he told me he didn't have a heart attack," Bush said while reassuring the nation about his running mate. "He's fit to serve and ready to be the next vice president of the United States."

The fact that Cheney was hospitalized was not that huge of a deal. But in the post-election public relations battle, Democrats used his hospitalization as another point of weakness on which to attack Bush. Bush didn't help himself in rushing to announce that his running mate didn't have a heart attack. Cheney did indeed have a minor heart attack that required the insertion of a stint in his heart. This caused more uproar with Democrats who accused Bush of trying to hide the truth about Cheney's condition.

While Bush may have been too eager to dispel rumors, it was Cheney himself who told Bush he didn't have a heart attack. He was simply passing on the information available at the time. But due to the pressures mounting for a resolution in the election fiasco, Bush was quick to spread some good news. In the end, it didn't sway the pendulum either way.

4:35 p.m. PST

In some ways, I guess it was seen as a small victory for Bush. Heavily Democratic Miami-Dade County, one of Gore's primary targets for his selective recounts, suddenly decided not to conduct a full manual recount due to one factor: time.

Despite the Florida Supreme Court's extension of the legal deadline to certify votes in Florida, Miami-Dade simply stated there was no possible way to count all the ballots and make the deadline. Instead, they decided to conduct a partial manual recount of some 10,000 "undervotes". These undervotes included ballots with no clear vote for president or perhaps two votes for president or what they called at the time "dimpled chads." Those were ballots where someone may have made an impression on a ballot but didn't completely punch it out.

This absolutely drove me crazy. Suddenly, the Democrats wanted election volunteers, who were mostly Democrats, to judge the intent of the voter. They, in essence, were being asked to read the mind of a voter who cast a ballot some three weeks earlier. It was a ludicrous notion that the Gore campaign argued for at nausea. They believed the law was on their side to judge what the intent of the voter was to ensure each "vote" was counted. This half-baked theory gained steam and Miami-Dade prepared to start its selective recount despite vehement opposition by the Bush team and Republicans.

But hold the phone. Out of nowhere, Miami-Dade then announces it will not conduct the partial manual recount in a 2-1 vote of its Democratic canvassing committee. Democrats quickly go on television to blame a "mob" of Republicans who had staged a demonstration inside the Miami-Dade election offices after election officials attempted to count ballots behind closed doors without observers and members of the media looking on.

"It's about time Republican's used some of the Democrat's tactics against them," I said to my wife that evening. "What kills me is they are acting like these people were rioting when it was 10-15 people. The hypocrisy is amazing."

"Of course. It's a bunch of Republicans so suddenly its intimidation," Eliete said. "But Jesse Jackson demonstrating on the street is not intimidation. There's no difference. They're just angry because they are starting to lose."

My wife's assessment was a good one but was Gore and the screaming Democrats really starting to lose? It sure seemed that way but the hills and valleys of Election 2000 made me second-guess just about everything that happened. I thought for sure the election was over after Gore lost in Florida Superior Court. Then the Florida Supreme Court jumped in and there went that. But the tide seemed to be changing. The PR battle was going Bush's' way and the American people seemed to be souring on Gore's fight. The Democratic core was staying true but there were rumblings that Democrats were about to jump ship.

There was no doubt the halting of the count in Miami-Dade County was a massive blow to Gore. They knew, or at least believed, they could pick up enough votes to overcome Bush. They just needed to votes counted and they were banking on their fellow Democrats to go to bat for them. When that didn't happen, Daley and Gore did what they did best: sue in court.

Gore sued Miami-Dade County to count the votes. In their legal opinion, they were required to do so. Gore, perhaps taking a queue from his boss of eight years Bill Clinton, turned to some friendlies. He filed a petition with the Florida Supreme Court asking they require Miami-Dade to recount the votes manually. Gore figured he could go back to the well and trust his case in the activist Democrats who had already thrown him a lifeline.

But the counting stopped and Bush took his fight to the U.S. Supreme Court to throw out hand counts all together. That was still pending but most legal experts agreed the chances of the U.S. Supreme Court hearing the case was slim and none. Most media outlets decried Bush's decision to take his case to the highest court of the land calling it a state's rights issue. In fact, the court in general was big on state's rights and most believed they would hold to that. But Republicans and Bush had faith in the system. Faith in a system that is required to rule based on law; not on petty partisan politics.

TWELVE
Thanksgiving, Turkeys & The Turning Tide

November 23

I remember the first image I woke up to on Thanksgiving Day 2000. It was Al Gore on television and I simply pointed at the television and said "See, it's turkey day."

Two major cases were pending over the holiday and although I was taking a self-imposed break from following the election, I still flipped to the news channels to check in just in case. With Gore's petition in front of the Florida Supreme Court, and the nation still waiting to hear if Bush would have his day in front of The Big Court, I settled in for a nice family Thanksgiving filled with football, food and the usual relaxed atmosphere.

As I delighted in spending time with my daughter Alexis and Eliete, the election and battle for America's pride was still in my mind. I couldn't get it out of my head or my gut. The Florida Supreme Court was at work. Would they again give Gore the relief he sought? Or would they do what they should have done in the first place and uphold the law of Florida?

Later in the day we found out.

The news flash came across the screen as a Fox News Channel anchor discussed the election happenings. The Florida Supreme Court had denied Gore's request to force Miami-Dade to continue the count. Although Gore was picking up votes in other counties, it was a harsh decision that threatened to completely torpedo Gore's ability to hang on any longer. The discussion turned to concession and of Democrats abandoning their man. The talk was that Gore wouldn't be able to get enough votes and this could perhaps end his lifelong quest to become president.

As the day came to a close, and the triptiphan kicked in rendering most of the Gulbransens to useless couch potatoes, I felt good for once about the chance that Bush may take this thing again. He had won twice already and now the ball seemed to be rolling his way.

I kissed my wife, daughter and new son and went on to worry about more practical things It was a good day and the world seemed just.

November 24

You have to love validation.

One day after the Florida Supreme Court ruled against Gore, the U.S. Supreme Court shocked the nation by agreeing to hear the petition of Bush regarding the Constitutionality of hand recounts in Florida. To say this was a surprise, even to us hearty Republicans, would be a massive understatement. The Court agreed to hear Bush's case, and Gore's rebuttal, on December 1st that meant we had to endure at least another week of the election drama. Despite the extension of this hoax, it felt good to have what seemed to be an impartial body's willingness to look at the case and decide once and for all who had won and what man would be regarded as the 43rd President of the United States.

That was all. Just that massively huge decision on this day. Finally, a day without a massive tug of war. I was one day away from turning 31 and felt as though the country was moving toward the direction I believed was right.

November 25

My birthday.

It was the usual: cake, candles, cards, gifts and the feeling that life was starting to move much too quickly.

On the election front, nothing worth mentioning happened. Just a bunch of talking heads spouting their beliefs on television. I bet they all write books.

November 26

It was deadline day and it wasn't clear if America's favorite county, Palm Beach, would conclude their recount in time to meet the Florida Supreme Court's imposed deadline of 5 p.m.

As the day wore on, it was evident they would not complete the count they fought so hard to keep going. No county as much as Palm Beach County represented what was fundamentally wrong with the process unfolding in Florida. The Democratic canvassing board an several of its members were so politically motivated, and enjoyed the face time on national television, they lost sight of what the goal truly was. It became about imposing their will on the American people instead of obeying what the true will was.

I won't mention their names because it validates their claim to fame and I don't want any part of that. The older female commissioner was perhaps the most bitter and backward thinking politician I have ever witnessed. She alone caused my blood pressure to rise. Anytime sheer ignorance is present I get hot.

Because they had take Thanksgiving off, while other counties decided to work through the holiday, they couldn't finish what they started. Instead, they filed a letter with Katherine Harris to extend the deadline. They were in essence asking for an extension to the extension.

Hello? Earth to Palm Beach County!

At the same time that Palm Beach County was attempting to pull its collective head out of its rectum, Broward County had finished its recount and Gore had picked up 500 votes. Imagine that. Throughout all these hand counts, it was always Gore that picked up massive amounts of votes. In my mind, putting aside my political views, these massive landslide gains were troublesome. Imagine watching a football game and every time a penalty flag is thrown, it's on one team. That's what was happening with the Florida vote. I couldn't believe the American people were being fooled by this orchestrated effort to manufacture votes for Gore.

Nonetheless, Bush maintained his lead, no matter how thin and at 5 p.m. EST, Harris declared Bush the winner of Florida by 537 votes.

At the same time, The Palm Beach Stooges continued to complain and threaten lawsuits. Their attempt to come through for Gore was thwarted and they didn't like it one bit. They used the face time to bash Katherine Harris and accuse her of being "politically motivated." As if they weren't doing the same thing? Hypocrisy should be the Democratic Party's slogan.

Later than evening, Gore's running mate, Senator Joe Lieberman, made an ass out of himself claiming the winner of Florida "must be decided by the person who received the most votes." Now there's a concept. Bush had now won three separate tallies of the votes in Florida but here is Lieberman on my television telling me the real winner is the man with the most votes. I'm sorry but how asinine can you get? Lieberman really hurt his credibility late in the election battle and the effects of that will no be known for years.

November 27

Sensing that the U.S.S. Gore was taking on tons of water from his battle over the holiday weekend, the vice-president reached out to Democratic leaders on Capital Hill to ensure their continued support. It was such an awkward and surreal photo opportunity it still makes me laugh to look back at it. Gore and Lieberman are on a telephone from the vice-president's residence and are discussing these issues with Senator Richard Gephardt and Tom Dashcle while the media listens in. It seemed as though the political robot was losing his grip.

But the unifying tone of the call helped Gore overall. Even though some behind the scenes may have been questioning Gore's desire to fight on, no one would say so publicly and the fight seemed to strengthen the resolved of many a Democrat.

This call occurs simultaneously as Gore files papers in Florida to officially contest the election results.

I've mentioned previously the 1960 election and how close it was. Richard Nixon, dejected after losing, was patriotic enough not to challenge the results and subject the American people to a crisis of unseen proportions. Nixon would eventually cause that himself but in 1960 he believed losing was an acceptable bitter pill to swallow to save America a major headache.

Gore couldn't bring himself to be the man Nixon was. He truly believed he had won Florida and, by contesting the election, aimed to prove it. He wanted to votes counted but was fine with military ballots being tossed out on technicalities. But in doing so, he risked dragging the nation through more ugliness.

I'd be lying if I didn't respect a portion of his feelings. I can understand if you feel you've been wronged. When that happens, you want to do everything humanly possible to prove what you believe is right. The analogy of being accused of a crime you didn't commit comes to mind. But with Gore, it was hard to feel sorry. He was cocky and didn't believe Bush could beat him to begin with. His fight was more about denial than proving himself a patriot. And the nation was starting to tire of the Gore way.

5:36 p.m. PST

As I sat down for dinner, looking at my children and how fast they seem to grow, the election mess continued to play out on the television. I was now interviewing for a new job so my stress level was rising a bit. My agency job wasn't all that I thought it would be and I decided to look elsewhere.

As I chowed down on my wife's homemade meal, my head turned toward the television with word that America's highest ranking robot would soon make a public statement.

"Not again," Eliete said.

"I don't understand why he feels the need to keep making these statements," I said. "Look at Bush. He's not made a public appearance in a while and when he does, he's working. The whole idea of Gore constantly being out there is a bad PR move. I'm telling you, he'll regret it."

"Scott, he's begging. He needs to be out there. He's completely in denial," Eliete said.

If it seems like our conversations seem a bit common, they were. Over and over again we had to discuss the same issues. We both seemed to get it but for some reason at least half of Americans somehow bought into this idea that Bush, not Gore, was stealing the election.

As his stiff torso made its way to the podium in front of his Washington residence, Al Gore looked like a cadaver. Not only was his expression stilted, but also his eyes lacked passion and conviction. I have never liked the man but being a political observer and keeping a keen eye on anything related to public relations, I watched Gore with as an objective view as I could.

"It is vital that all the votes in Florida be counted," Gore said. "We have never asked for anything more or anything less than a fair and accurate count."

The mantra, again and again. To their credit, the Gore team stuck to their key messages and hammered them home daily in a variety of venues. This was a smart public relations strategy and it seemed to be working on one level. Many Americans, mostly Democrats and those important swing voters who sometimes cross party lines to vote for a candidate based on issues, believed that every vote must be counted; even if cast incorrectly.

Now I ask you; if you cannot vote correctly, then your vote has no right to be counted. Voting is a right of every American not convicted of a felony. But in the Florida melee, even convicts were allowed to vote for Gore even though they were excluded under Florida law. But when these stories somehow made it through the overwhelmingly pro-Gore television media, they somehow were brushed off very quickly.

As we prepared to put the kids to bed, I turned to my wife and felt the need to express myself again. We were together in this election mess and it had opened our eyes further.

"Elie?"

"Yes, Scott."

"I'm telling you, if Gore steals this thing, we're all in a lot of trouble. I'm trying to look at this from a pure legal and Constitutional view and I can't understand how people are being fooled. Am I just being a strong Republican here? Or is what I am saying making sense?"

My wife, in her infinite wisdom, gave me the comforting answer I was looking for. "Scott, people today have lost a sense of reality. No one wants to stand up and be responsible for his or her actions. Look at parents and what they allow their children to get away with. People today know less about their own system of government than half the immigrants that come into this country each day. They're all too sensitive and they want to impose their will on everyone while accusing Republicans of doing the same thing. It's the most hypocritical view I've ever seen."

Wow.

My wife is a strong woman with strong opinions. Being just on generation removed from immigrant parents who fled Cuba to come America, she fits the profile of many Democrats. Female, Hispanic and young. But she has a great head on her shoulders and she too understood what was happening.

November 28

The watershed event on this day was really the Bush team's preparation of their appeal for the U.S. Supreme Court. Lead Bush attorney, Ted Olsen, who would later lose his wife Nancy in the September 11th hijackings, had to make a compelling argument that the Florida Supreme Court interpreted the U.S. Constitution incorrectly when allowing manual recounts to continue. This argument would be difficult because Olsen would have to prove that the Florida court violated due process in rendering their decision. No one really gave Bush a chance when he petitioned the Supreme Court and now, they were predicting the court would not rule for Bush instead upholding the state law.

The argument was only three days away but insiders were telling the media the Bush team was making good progress and felt good about their chances. The attention quickly shifted to the nine U.S. Supreme Court Justices and their individual political views. The court, still with what most would consider a "conservative" bent, was a court that upheld the rights of State's to govern themselves. They were a court usually in tandem with one another when it comes to state issues. It was easy to see why the so-called experts believe they would uphold the Florida decision.

By the middle of the day, fearing what an argument in front of the nation's highest court may mean, the Gore team filed a motion to have the case dismissed from the Supreme Court docket. Gore's attorneys argued the issues was for a state court to decide and that a federal court had no jurisdiction in the matter. The argument was a strong one but most legal experts agreed it really had no chance of getting the Supreme Court out of the game.

The Supreme Court would deny the Gore request and both sides readied for their arguments.

Noon PST

I remember going to lunch and running to a local grocery store to pick up a few items. The conversation everywhere related to the election. I heard pro-Gore comments and just as many pro-Bush comments from fellow shoppers and employees at the chain supermarket.

"I just can't wait until Bush loses," the middle-aged woman a few people in front of me said. "He's a crook and a cocaine user. How could anyone vote for him?"

Now, usually, in a public place, I bite my tongue and just right off comments like that to the lack of brain cells some of us are cursed with in life. But this time, I had to say something. This election had become such a part of my daily life, I felt the need to fire back.

"I guess for the same reason they'd vote for a pervert who constantly cheats on his wife and then lies in court about it," I said with a smile.

She said nothing. She was shocked. She just rolled her eyes at the clerk and made her way to her new Range

Rover in the parking lot. I assumed her life was pretty much empty and that her husband probably cheated on her too so she was accepting of Clinton's indiscretions. These pessimistic and bordering on mean thoughts had boiled over in recent weeks. I shouldn't judge people but the amazing double standard was wearing thin on me.

2:30 p.m.

The double standard again raised its ugly head. Robert Litt and I were about to exchange another email. The young Democrat was responding to a note I sent him on a joke related to Clinton's sex scandal.

——Original Message——
From: Robert Litt
Sent: Tuesday, November 28, 2000 2:30 PM
 To: Scott Gulbransen
 Subject: RE: Your Boy!

I rather have a president who had a blowjob in the oval office than a president who snorts cocaine and gets arrested for a DWI....

Now, I've told you earlier in this book how much I think of young Rob and his future in the public relations field. But in his writing you could see clearly the double standard I was referring to when arguing with the woman in the grocery store. After all, liberalism is a mental disorder. Both times Bush was attacked for cocaine use when no one ever proved he had used the drug. Most had assumed the answer was yes since Bush refused to answer the question. But the dirt against Clinton and Gore was proven with evidence. Clinton had done everything he was accused of related to Lewinsky and Gore and raised campaign funds with the help of Chinese nationals. This attack on Bush was groundless because it had no proof. Perhaps Bush, in the throws of youth, had used cocaine but no one could come forward and offer evidence to support the accusation. That bothered Democrats who couldn't find anything but a 27 year-old traffic ticket that showed Bush had been driving when he shouldn't have after too many drinks.

I'm not downplaying Bush's culpability in driving drunk; it's a serious offense he committed when he was a young man. But to compare that with getting oral sex in the White House and lying to a Grand Jury is plain ridiculous.

Sure, Republicans have had their incidents too. Humans make mistakes no matter what position in life they hold. That's part of life. But it seems the Democrats try to complete destroy the character of a person when they make an error in judgment but when a Democrat does the same thing, we should all forgive them. I don't understand that logic.

Gore's big gun legally throughout the process had been David Boies. The same attorney who led the government's attack on Bill Gates and Microsoft was not trying to help his buddy Gore sue to the White House.

As many news sources reported during the election fiasco, Boies, a big shot New York attorney, broke the law and lied to the Florida Supreme Court misleading them on several key issues. Add to that the fact he wasn't licensed to practice in Florida and you can see why he was a decisive figure.

On November 28, I had had enough of Boies and his anti-American views. That day, on the Strategic Jungle, I wrote this column:

Counsel to the New World Order
Just call him attorney for the New World Order.

Lead Al Gore henchmen David Boies remains in Florida trying in earnest to steal the election from George W. Bush and crush the very will of the people he so often says he is defending. Yet it should come as no surprise that Boies would be the driving force behind diluting and destroying democracy in America.

When the Clinton administration decided to go head·on with Microsoft, David Boies was the first to step forward. By anyone's account, Boies is a brilliant lawyer who has earned a reputation as a highly intelligent and effective barrister. Gore may be the stiffest and most android like politician in America today but he knew what he was doing when he chose his legal general.

But if you look at the Microsoft case that Boies prosecuted, and what he is currently up to in Florida, it's easy to see his agenda is the same as Clinton, Gore and all Democrats who seek to change our system by changing its law in the courtroom.

Today's America lacks many of the business savvy we held just 40 years ago. No longer are we a country with a large manufacturing base capable of shipping goods throughout the world to countries in need or want of our labor. Instead, through NAFTA and other treasonous agreements with foreign nations, the United States faces a trade deficit like never before.

By far the one product and company who has done the most for the American economy over the past 20 years has been Microsoft and it's operating system and family of software. Like him or hate him, Bill Gates is a brilliant businessman who reshaped the economy of this nation. Along side several of the large computer manufacturers like Dell and Gateway, Microsoft's climb and maintenance of its place in the market is unrivaled. In a country where the word "monopoly" is tossed around like fraudulent ballots in Broward Country, Clinton and Gore knew they had to take out Gates and his company to strip America of its one true product · software. If they could, their dreams of a one-world government and the fall of America's border would be just around the corner.

At the center of all this is Boies. He prosecuted the Microsoft case and continues to be the bagman for the Clinton Gore Machine. He's almost succeeded in destroying this nation's best and brightest corporation and now he seeks to overturn the will of the people by stealing the 2000 election.

Although Boies comes across as bright, articulate and calm on television, many of those inside the Gore campaign say he sometimes loses sight of the cause when trying to win. That's where we are at right now. Gore knows he lost. Despite campaign aides stating Gore believes he won Florida, he's never been his own man. This fight is not about Gore vs. Bush. It's Boies versus democracy. Boies wants so badly to win and run the table in the courts he doesn't care what happens to the nation or his candidate. Gore knows he should fall on his sword but Boies keeps pulling the sword from his hands.

Most would have you believe that Boies is just a lawyer trying to win at all costs. That is true to a degree but even though he has represented companies like IBM and even the music-swapping site Napster, Boies is always there, trying to tear down, not build up. He has a fundamental problem with the system and laws that govern our society. He has shown over the years his desire to be the "rebel" and change the course of our democracy.

There is no question this country has grown tired of this seesaw battle of the lawyers in Florida. Today's latest Gallup Poll says 56 percent of Americans believe Gore should concede. But the inmates are running the prison. David Boies is the lead prisoner and he won't stop as long as the fees keep rolling in.

Boies is not doing this because he believes Gore won. He's doing it because he is deathly afraid of a Republican administration that would push tort reform. The only thing really important to Boies is his wallet.

Sadly, he's willing to destroy our nation in order to fill it.

6:07 p.m. PST

Fox News Channel again. It was time for my nightly briefing via Hannity and Colmes, Bill O'Reilly and Paula Zahn. The news on this evening was the move by the Florida Legislature to start discussing the election of pro-Bush electors should the mess carry on past December 18. This would only be done if the state felt their representation at the meeting of the Electoral College would be in danger.

It was another move Daley and Gore hadn't counted on. Just as they overlooked Harris, they too overlooked the Republican controlled government of Florida. The Democrats seemed to be running out of options but the fight was far from over.

November 29

One thing was becoming crystal clear to America and the Gore campaign: time was running out. The longer the legal wrangling dragged on, the slimmer the hope that Gore would become the 43rd President of the United States. As time marched toward the December 18th Electoral College deadline, time to recount votes was falling through the hands of Boies, Gore, Daley, et al. This was so clear to me, I penned another column about Bush and his best friend, the clock:

Court Battle May Be Moot as Clock Favors Bush

If you listen closely today, you may hear George W. Bush humming under his breath the Rolling Stones classic tune "Time is on My Side."

Although a selfish and defiant Al Gore continues to try and overturn the results of the election in Florida, the clock is ticking and there are only a few seconds left. He knows it. His lawyers know it and soon they will panic.

Throughout Tuesday, Gore's army of attorneys continued to spread half-truths and lies concerning the election results in Florida. Not only that, they continue to assert Bush is attempting to delay court actions so the "clock runs out."

Well, DUH!

The whole idea that the judicial system in this country should rush through normal procedures and timetables is ludicrous. It is true the Presidency is at stake but there is no reason to rush since Bush is the legal winner of the state of Florida, and by law, the President-elect of the

United States. Gore wants only to prolong the process so he can commit the most egregious theft in U.S. history.

Friday, when both camps make their case in front of this nation's highest court, the outcome and public reaction to it could swing the pendulum either way. Most legal experts agree that even if Bush "loses" in the U.S. Supreme Court, he probably will beat Gore in Florida court. The Florida court is stacked with Democrats who are desperately attempting to rewrite the laws of the state to favor their Robot in Chief but the clock does favor Bush.

During this whole "broken" election, a slanted media has constantly bombarded us. They have constantly looked to give the Veep any advantage. With the exception of perhaps Fox News Channel, most national networks continue to spew pro-Gore rhetoric. They too would like to prolong this national embarrassment because ad revenues are climbing and they are enjoying their highest ratings ever.

Despite the strength of the national liberal media, and their stranglehold on this election, they too are running out of time.

What makes these legal wranglings a moot point is the second wild card the pit bull Dems never counted on - the Florida Legislature. Just as they assumed Secretary of State Katherine Harris would not go against their stacked political machine, they forgot about the lawmakers of Florida and how Republicans controlled the body. No matter what happens in the hollowed judicial halls of the Sunshine State this week, the Florida Legislature will choose Bush delegates. When that happens, Bush will have the needed 270 Electoral College votes he needs to become the President.

If Florida is still in dispute, the United States Congress will be asked to decide which Electors from Florida to accept. If we've gotten to that point, we're all in trouble and the much-discussed Constitutional crisis so often bantered around by lawyers and experts on the boob-tube over the past three weeks will be upon us.

That is why, again, Gore must be pressured to concede. The latest round of public opinion polls show an overwhelming majority of Americans want Gore to give up the fight and allow this nation to move forward. Gore said yesterday it was a legal issue now and not one of public opinion. That's rather funny coming from the mouth of a man who constantly reminds us he won the popular vote. It appears Gore cares about public opinion only when it favors his slanted, liberal views.

I have a slew of heavily Democratic colleagues who I have talked to throughout the process. They would defend Gore to the death. But after Sunday, even they agree its time to throw in the towel and live to fight another day. Gore doesn't see that and is quickly committing political suicide that will cost him his chances for the Democratic nomination in 2004.

So, my fellow tired and angry conservatives fear not. This long election nightmare is soon to end and the man who is our next President, George W. Bush, will soon move into 1600 West Pennsylvania Avenue.

THIRTEEN

A Supreme Argument

December 1

The week was ending with a few more developments than normal. Then again, what the hell was normal about this election?

With a hearing set to take place on December 2nd related to Gore's official contest of the entire Florida election, Washington D.C. was buzzing as attorneys for both sides were about to argue their case to the U.S. Supreme Court. Again, the issue revolved around Florida's Supreme Court and their decision to allow manual recounts after a deadline past which was enforced by Florida statute. Bush attorney Ted Olson had to sway the court to believe Bush's Constitutional rights to due process were violated, which made the issue federal thereby deserving of some remedy of the U.S. Court.

Gore attorney Laurence Tribe, a Harvard law professor, argued that the issue was strictly a state issue and should have never left the state and made its way into a federal court. Tribe contended the Florida Supreme Court was compelled to interpret the state law to ensure the rights of individual voters was not violated. It was a simple argument that wouldn't need much support but still nothing was for sure.

7 a.m. PST

The arguments had begun but because the U.S. Supreme Court doesn't allow cameras, America would have to wait to hear how the fight went. The Court, realizing the immense public interest in the case, agreed to have an audio recording made of the arguments that would be released with 30 minutes after the session had concluded.

As I raced for work, I listened to news radio waiting for reports from journalists who were going in and out to report on happenings so far. The first update came after 10 minutes and just discussed the argument of Olson on behalf of Bush. I just wanted to get to work so I could listen to the audio once it was released.

Soon after the audio was release, I dialed in CNN.com and cued up the recording. It was a surreal experience listening to the proceedings unfold. My ears were alive much like the first time I listened to old radio shows from the 1930s and 1940s. I could almost imagine my Dad listening to "Gangbusters" or "The Shadow" with the same excitement I listened to the first audio recording of the United States Supreme Court.

I was of course at work so I could not listen to the entire proceeding but was doing my best to hear what I needed to hear. I also knew there would be thousands of reports later in the day comparing the two arguments trying to gauge who had won and what the court would decide. It was Hollywood drama. With all due respect to Humphrey Bogart, this was the best movie I had ever watched and the actors were all stellar. If you tried to pitch the story, people would laugh in your face. It was fantasy that became reality and I was living it.

Throughout the day, as the battle raged on in Washington, several other key legal challenges were being mounted:

▶ In preparation for the contest hearing in front of Florida judge Sanders Sauls, over 1 million ballots are shipped via Ryder truck to Tallahassee to be on hand should more counts be ordered. The ballots were brought to the capital under armed guard to ensure their security.

▶ Bush and his attorneys file a new motion with Sauls to dismiss the Gore contest contending that Gore's actions were baseless since neither presidential candidate was really on the ballot. Bush argued Floridians were really casting votes for electors whom neither Gore nor Bush had the right to speak for. It was a long shot but the Republicans needed to slow down the process.

▶ The Florida Supreme Court, much to everyone's surprise, rejects the Gore appeal to immediately begin a manual recount of some 14,000 ballots in dispute. This makes Gore's contest of the election more difficult as it puts it into the hands of the lower courts and not the activist Florida Supreme Court.

▶ Later in the evening, the Florida Supreme Court again rejects a Gore appeal asking for a revote in Palm Beach County. This inflames Jesse Jackson who has been screaming racial injustice since the first day of the contested election. This, in essence, puts to bed the "butterfly ballot" issue once and for all.

This legal battleground was making my head spin. I was monitoring the situation constantly but the events of December 1st were both exhilarating and exhausting. Since I had since an intense interest in the outcome of the broken election, I experienced first-hand its ups and downs.

7:02 pm.

Listening to the accounts of the days legal motions and hearing the experts argue back and forth about who had the upper hand, I came to a frightening realization; we were no closer than we were on November 8 of finding out who our president would be. That was deflating and it was taking its toll on my physical well being.

Earlier in the day, I had attended a party for my last day of work at the public relations firm I was working for. It was an awkward party but I was able to say goodbye to many people I had come to know in the short six months I had worked there. But throughout the event, my mind turned to the election. I was getting in way too deep but I couldn't help myself.

Sitting in our bedroom, I could barely move.

"What's wrong with you tonight,"Eliete asked.

"I'm just tired. The stress of starting a new job and this election is killing me. I don't know if I can explain it but I am living and dying with what happens ever day," I said.

Eliete reached over and rubbed my shoulders and kissed my forehead. She knew because, to a lesser degree, she was experiencing the same thing. It was something we stood side-by-side through and it would be something we'd talk about the rest of our lives. Hence this book.

As I sat in our dark room that night, I wondered what it all meant. What was the lesson of all this? How would it make America stronger? I didn't have the answers but I was willing to look for them. But with any historical event, only time can really reveal what, if anything, we learn from national experiences. Plus, it wasn't even over yet.

December 2-3

All weekend, Bush and Gore attorneys argued in front of Judge Sauls. The issue was the official contest of the election and whether there would be further counts. The hometown judge, Sauls, offered some hysterical moments during the two-day hearing. He was a good ol' boy and a Democrat but Gore attorney David Boies was getting nervous as were Democrats all over the nation. The arguments seemed to be going the Bush way and Gore's attorneys already discussed appealing to the Florida Supreme Court should Sauls rule against them. Since most lawyers are Democrats, and Clinton kept so many of them busy during his eight years in office, there answer for everything was to sue. And they were getting ready should things not go their way.

A nervous nation again waited for the other shoe to drop. When would the U.S. Supreme Court issue a ruling? Would they even issue a ruling? Would the ruling be strong enough to elicit a concession by one of the candidates?

These were all questions on the minds of Americans as Sunday came to a close.

December 4

Anticipation. That was the one word that cold describe the feeling of most people, including myself. The Supreme Court had review the case over the weekend and the sense was a decision would come soon. With reporters camped outside the building, shielding themselves from the Washington winter temperatures, everyone was on the edge of their seats.

I remained positive and was thinking the U.S. Supreme Court would rule for Bush and put an end to the fight. It seemed pretty reasonable that Bush's Constitutional rights had been violated and that the Florida Supreme Court had acted incorrectly when they allowed the recounts to go on past the deadline. End of story, thank you, good night President-elect Bush.

The day was not very old when the announcement came down: the Supreme Court was about to issue its ruling.

As I sat in front of the television waiting for the word, I got nervous. I was sure the Supreme Court would do what was right but would they? It was the ugly self-doubt monster crawling into my head. It had been such an up-and-down three weeks and most of us just wanted it to be over and Bush to win what was rightfully his.

As the opinion was read, the most disturbing feeling overcame me. Had the justices been playing football, their opinion on December 4th would have been the equivalent of punting the ball on third down. They had the opportunity to rule and perhaps end the election but instead, deferred to state's rights with a strong slap on the wrist.

In the seven page opinion (found at the end of this book in the legal documents section), the court stated it could not understand the reason the Florida Supreme Court ruled the way it did.

"After reviewing the opinion of the Florida Supreme Court, we find 'that there is considerable uncertainty as to the precise grounds for the decision,' *Minnesota v. National Tea Comp., 309 U.S. 501, 555 (1940).* This is sufficient for us to decline at this time to review the federal questions asserted to be present."

What? At first, it was a bit confusing. Here the Florida Supreme Court was being told by the U.S. Supreme Court that it couldn't understand why, and using what law, it ruled the way it did but yet it remanded the case back to them for clarification. This meant Bush's lead of 930 votes was reinstated and the Florida Court had to answer the Supreme Court with reasons why it ruled in Gore's favor.

In essence, we were back to square one again. No result. No end to the madness. Just more confusion.

At the time, I was very upset. I couldn't understand the court's desire to skirt the real issue at hand and leave the election decision up to a court of judges known for legislating from the bench. I was angry and was losing my patriotic bent I had always had the utmost respect for the U.S. Supreme Court and even that was eroding. I had a sense America was about to be torn apart and no one was willing to step forward to stop it.

"Elie? Did you hear?"

"Her what?"

"They sent the case back to Florida. Can you believe it? He's (Gore) going to do it Elie. Get ready to move to Italy," I said in haste.

I was upset and talking crap. really mean it though. I'm not like the bloated actor Alex Baldwin who, with several other high-profile celebrities, vowed to leave the United States if Bush were elected. I wasn't going to leave just solely because Gore was about to steal the election, for me it was more about the ignorance of many Americans and the crumbling legal system that would allow it. Those are the things that upset me. I don't like Gore but I wasn't about to move just because he won the White House, if he had won the White House. My issues were more centrally related to the Founding Fathers and their vision on what this country should be. It was about the trampling of our Constitution and what that meant for my children. I know that sounds a bit lofty but those were my emotions at the time.

Despite the wishy-washy ruling by the Supreme Court, the rest of the day would lift my spirits a little.

3:10 p.m. PST

Judge Sanders Sauls threw and uppercut that hit Gore in the nuts. He ruled there was not sufficient evidence to allow Gore to contest the election because the Gore attorneys had not shown any "proof of illegality, dishonesty, gross negligence, improper influence or fraud" in relation to voting in Florida.

This was a huge win for Bush but it was to be short lived as Boies and his army of attorneys marched across the street and filed an immediate appeal with the Florida Supreme Court asking that the contest be allowed to proceed.

Throughout the Sauls hearing, over two days, Boies and his attorneys were frustrated because the judge would not allow the ballots to be counted should Sauls agree with Gore and allow it to continue. They had a sense things would not go their way in his courtroom and, in my opinion, had decided to go to the Florida Supreme Court early on. They had friends there and they wanted the case to go there. It may have been a low blow for Gore but there was huge upside.

5:44 p.m. PST

As I ate dinner with my family, my stomach fluttered. It was going back to the Florida Supreme Court and I had no faith there would be a good result. The talking heads on television guessed the Florida Supreme Court would be extra careful after being "taken behind the shed" by their more powerful cousins in Washington. Others stated they would rule for Bush and end it all. But I knew better.

Whether your evaluating a stock, looking at the reliability of a car, or judging the actions of a human being, there's one telling way to see which way it will go: consistency.

The Florida Supreme Court was consistent alright. They constantly legislated from the bench and were willing to make political statements with their opinions. They were not a court strictly abiding by state law; they had an agenda and it was their desire to enforce that agenda and whatever should come before them. Many of my fellow conservatives didn't agree. They felt the game had come to an end. I wanted to agree with them but I felt they were merely attempting to fool themselves.

December 5

Eliete's birthday. Cake, card, presents, the usual. We had a nice time and my wife, living away from her native Las Vegas for the first time, missed her family. But we had each other, our beautiful children and the election to keep us busy.

Not surprising was the Florida Supreme Court's decision later in the day to hear Al Gore's appeal. Again proving their desire to soak in the limelight, the activist court opened the door and Gore, on the verge of being forced to concede, still had some gas in the tank.

The Florida court sets a date of Thursday, December 7th to hear oral arguments at the request of both parties wanting to resolve the issue. It benefits Gore to have a quick resolution because votes cannot be counted until the court rules one way or the other. So the Gore team, again snatching victory from the jaws of defeat, lives another day. But none of them looked surprised.

I am not going to imply a conspiracy theory but Boies and his legal eagles knew the Florida Supreme Court would act a certain way and they used that to their advantage. You'll never hear me say Boies is a bad attorney. He's a great attorney with no ethical map, in my opinion. But he always seemed to know what was going to happen before it did. I don't believe in coincidence do the idea that Boies had an "in" crossed my mind several times. All apologies to Mel Gibson.

4:49 p.m. PST

Flipping channels and all I see is Boies and Lieberman. Running the assault from two different fronts but preaching the same message.

"We've said all along that we felt the Florida Supreme Court would be the final arbiter in this case," Lieberman said from Washington appearing on NBC. "We'll abide by whatever the Florida court does and we feel they'll agree with us that all the votes must be counted."

Then it's Boies turn on Fox News Channel.

"Form the beginning we have said the Florida Supreme Court will make the final decision in this matter," Boies said to Fox host Brit Hume. "I still believe that today and that's where we are. Certainly we would have liked Judge Sauls' decision to go our way but we have been ready to go before the Florida Supreme Court with the case."

See? It's like he knew it would get back to his buddies in the Florida Supreme Court. When you know the route, you don't worry about the directions or mishaps along the way.

Meanwhile, Bush was busy getting his first Central Intelligence Agency briefing. Due to the lagging election controversy, the CIA felt it important to update Bush should be prevail. After all, the nation's security was of utmost interest to Bush and he needed to be prepared. Gore was receiving the same briefings in his current position as vice president but the public relations power of Bush receiving the briefings was good for his image. I will discuss the PR aspects later but the fact Bush looked and was acting presidential helped him during these confusing episodes. Bush had kept an overall low profile while Lieberman and Boies splashed themselves all over television the night of December 5th.

"What do you think will happen," I asked Eliete. "Are you kidding? They're going to rule for Gore," she said.

"How can they? The Supreme Court just spanked them. Do you still think they'll go with their guy."

"I'll tell you what, if they go against Bush again they're going to be telling the U.S. Supreme Court to go jump of a bridge and that's going to piss them off," Eliete said.

Now, my wife doesn't always curse, and I'm sure I'll hear about putting it in a book for all time, but she too was now lost in the emotion. We are so much a like and think alike her mind and my mind were on the same channel. But being who I am, I always try to wish away the stark reality of what lies ahead. Eliete was being a realist and I was being a optimist.

Normally, conversations like those listed above, might seem a bit on the boring side. After all, we kept asking each other the same questions. It goes to show you how much this was all engulfing our lives. It was like that throughout America - on both sides of the fences. oth sides feeling they were right and about to lose their grip.

As much as I think the Democrats are dead wrong, I do respect every American's right to think as they do and to believe in what they feel is right.

December 6

A down day in the crazy process. While both sides prepare their legal arguments and file them with the Florida Supreme Court, the Republican leaders of the Florida Legislature schedule a special session for Saturday the 8th to consider selecting their own pro-Bush electors.

Immediately the Democrats go on an all-out media blitz to deplore the action and charge the Republicans of Florida with circumventing the law. In reality, the Republicans were trying to ensure that the state of Florida was able to supply electors to cast votes in the 2000 presidential election. Was it politically motivated to help Bush? Sure it was. But that's what politics are all about. They're about wielding power to do what you think is best for your constituents. But Democrats had a rough time with that and fought tooth and nail to stop it via the media. But their message was hollow and didn't deter the Florida Legislature from moving forward.

The other, smaller legal cases involving military ballots and the Democratic suit alleging vote fraud were all being heard on this day too but they never had any bearing on the final outcome.

As the day closed, the focus turned toward trying to guess how both sides would argue the next day. By most accounts, it was Gore's team that would have the most difficult time based on the fact that Sauls had really done his homework and issued a judgment, which many felt was air tight.

FOURTEEN

Mr. Bush Goes to Washington – Sort of

December 7

Forever in my mind, I will associate December 7th with Pearl Harbor and the year 1941. The sneak attack by Japan against the United States thrust us into World War II changing the globe forever. I have always been a history buff and I found it ironic the Florida Supreme Court may be planning a torpedo run of their own on the day we honor the brave men and women who died in our first battle of World War II.

Unlike the U.S. Supreme Court, cameras were allowed inside the Florida State House to view the proceedings. Because Gore had filed the appeal, his attorneys presented their case first.

What did Gore need to prove? Boies basic argument centered on Saul's refusal to inspect any of the disputed ballots brought to Tallahassee before his hearing to listen to the Gore election contest. The Gore legal team said Sauls erred in not doing so and the only appropriate remedy was for the Florida Supreme Court to step in and resolve the election dispute. Again, the Gore group was asking of the ballots to be counted. Even though they had already been tallied three times.

The Bush team had an easier battle. They had to use law to prove that Sauls ruled correctly in seeing their was no reason to think any fraud or deception, which needed to be proven under Florida law to contest an election, had occurred. The basic argument was for the Florida Supreme Court to stay out of the matter. Saul's decision was based on strong interpretation of Florida law and Bush argued it should end there.

The arguments seemed to be very balanced. Both attorneys did a fine job in presenting their case. The Florida justices seemed to be pro-Gore again in their line of questioning but there was no real way to know what they were going to do. As the arguments concluded, and the a respective attorneys had their press conferences, there was Boies, cool as ice again. To this day, I am convinced he knew he had won. Not a hunch but he knew the court was again rule against Florida law. It was a pattern behavior for them and he was using it for Gore. I had a conversation with my father that night. He felt it was over and the Florida Supreme Court wouldn't dare spit in the face of the U.S. Supreme Court by ruling again for Gore ensuring another session before them.

"There's no way they are going to do it again," he said.

"Don't be so sure, Dad. These judges don't care. They want to rewrite the law and they want to do it with their decisions. I think Bush will win but look what the last three weeks have been like. I'm tired of it."

My frustration was wearing on me. The weeks of following the election so closely were catching up. I wasn't sleeping well, I wasn't eating well and I was addicted to watching television coverage of the events. I've never been addicted to drugs or alcohol but I could feel the stress of feeling as though you had to have something every day. I had to have my election fix and I wanted it so badly to go the way *I* thought it should go. It's as though I had take ownership of it. It was my election and everyone else would have to see me about it.

I know that sounds crazy but I had become more emotionally attached. I have always tried to keep emotion out of my political discussions and observations because your head is more clear if you keep your emotions in check. But there I was, a mess. Waiting for the most ridiculous court in America to give Al Gore the election. I didn't want it to happened and spent quite a bit of time convincing myself it wouldn't but doubt came charging at me again.

December 8

December 8th will be looked upon as the day things changed dramatically, yet again, in the 2000 election. The country waited for any word out of Florida. What would the Florida Supreme Court do? They were quick to answer and their answer was horrific.

Afternoon

The events started unfolding so quickly, there were new developments every five minutes. The decision was reached and handed to the court clerk. The Florida Supreme Court again threw a lifeline to Al Gore by ordering the following:

• An immediate manual recount of every undervote in all of Florida's 67 counties. That meant a complete manual recount of the entire state.

• The court added 383 votes to Gore's tally reinstating the recounted votes the U.S. Supreme Court had stripped from the Vice President only days earlier. This cut Bush's lead to just 154 votes.

Never in my wildest dreams did I think the Florida Supreme Court would act so brazen and without regard for the law they were entrusted to keep. I became physically ill as a nauseous feeling overcame my stomach. It was the first time in my life I want to take to the streets and protest the destruction of our Constitution and legal system by a group of judges bent on proving a point. I was fed up and wanted out of America. I never thought I would feel that way but I truly wanted out. I wanted out of a country that would throw away its laws to serve a political purpose. It was a sad day for me and I would never forget that feeling. Writing this makes me feel it all over again.

Not only did they ignore Florida law, but the justices added votes the U.S. Supreme Court had taken away. It was outright theft. The court has no power to award votes in any election. How was it possible for these judges to do this and sleep that night. It was treasonous and I was angry.

Here were my immediate thoughts and the column I filed for the *Strategic Jungle Syndicate*:

Florida Court Tramples US Constitution

Someone wake me up.

Some how I went to sleep in America and woke up in a Third World country. Suddenly our governing document, the United States Constitution, was completely trampled on and effectively used as toilet paper by liberal justices inside the Florida Supreme Court.

Make no bones about it; our very democracy and way of governing is under full-fledged attack by those more interested in keeping power than the best interests of our country.

The one emotion that comes to the forefront of my entire being is anger. This is not because I believe so much that George W. Bush would be the best man to lead our nation but because he has won this election fair and square.

I had faith that the Florida court, already spanked by the large hand of the U.S. Supreme Court, would come to their senses and rule by the law. Instead, they shoved their noses at the highest court in the land and insulted each and every American. Including those Americans who died for this nation on the battlefields of Georgia to the killing fields of Vietnam.

There is no doubt in my mind that the U.S. Supreme
Court must take hold of this renegade court and uphold
the finding of Judge Sauls. During this election, we have
been shocked by the seemingly unending surprises but
rest assured those surprises will end once the highest
court strikes down this illegal and treasonous finding by
the biggest joke of a court in our nation.

The finding today by the Florida Supreme Court refused
to answer the questions posed by the U.S. Supreme Court
when it vacated its November 21st decision. Not only that,
the court extended its own deadline of November 25 to
count all the votes and certify them with the Secretary of
State. Not only did it spit on the U.S. Constitution, but it
also ran rough shot over its previous decision. Apparently,
the Florida Court "jesters" decided they could extend the
deadline yet again possibly throwing the entire nation
into a Constitutional crisis.

But just as Al Gore only cares about his own ego and
aspirations, so to does the four members of the Florida
Supreme Court that voted to overturn the Leon County
ruling. The only good coming from this decision is the
words of the Chief Justice of Florida. The fact the head of
the court wrote and signed the dissention, says a lot.
Court followers said late Friday that never happens.

The next few days will decide if we live in a country that
even resembles that constructed by our founding fathers.
This is the real deal folks, it's time to fight for what is
right.

In the mean time, I am packing the boxes and a move to
Italy might just be in order.

I was speechless and didn't even say anything to my wife. We both felt the same way. There was no need to put to words what was swirling in our heads. We both felt abandoned by America and I could only hope a miracle or someone with sense would jump in and change the outcome. Almost child-like was my denial and reassurance to myself a miracle would save us from this self-destruction.

Bush would immediately appeal to the Supreme Court but they would be of no help. They'd probably punt it again. But there was some hope, no matter how small.

As both campaigns geared for more recounts, I could only sit and watch with a glazed look in my eye. I felt like Jack Nicholson in *One Flew Over the CooCoo's Nest* – after the lobotomy.

December 9

It was Saturday morning and waking up after the one day I had slept in that month, I flipped on the TV. Live pictures of elections officials in all of Florida's 67 counties discussing how to move forward with the recounts ordered the previous day were taking place. It was like watching a bunch of rats in a maze. All the Florida Supreme Court had done, besides raising its middle finger at the U.S. Supreme Court, was add to the confusion.

How should the ballots be counted? What constitutes a vote? Do you count hanging chads? What about dimpled chads?

It was again time to write a column for the *Strategic Jungle Syndicate*. By my tone, you can tell just how dejected I was:

US Supreme Court May Offer No Help for Bush

With Al Gore's theft of the U.S. presidency one step close to reality, don't expect the U.S. Supreme Court to go the GOP way.

Almost immediately after the Florida Supreme Court's abominable decision yesterday, Bush attorneys rushed a request for a stay to Supreme Court Justice Anthony Kennedy in the hopes the counting would be stopped before it begun. Now, almost 16 hours later, the justice and the Supreme Court remain eerily silent.

Many observers expected Kennedy may react quickly to Bush's request since the justice's questions the first time around seemed to cast doubt on what the Florida court decided back on November 21. Kennedy was appointed by Reagan and is one of the court's solid conservative members.

But Kennedy's lack of response should send a clear signal to all of us that Al Gore may just get away with the most egregious election fraud in U.S. history. A theft helped along by an activist court bent on enforcing its will on the entire nation.

After yesterday's surreal events, conventional wisdom led most Republicans to think the U.S. Supreme Court, already haven rebuked the Florida court last month, would come out harsh against the fraudulent justices in Tallahassee. But here we are Saturday morning and still no word from the highest court. They obviously don't see any reason to hurry or at least grant Bush a stay until the confusion subsides.

The silence of the Supreme Court should be alarming to all Americans. Watching live broadcasts of the vote recounts in Florida this morning should petrify even the staunchest Democrat. They can't even decide how to get the under votes out of piles of normal votes and then have to decide which votes to count.

We have the Florida Supreme Court to thank for this mess. They rule to count all these votes but give no fair and equitable system to count them. That is irresponsible and reckless.

So, again, the nation waits. As we have done for a month since Election Day, we sit and let the attorneys decide who will be our next president.

Meanwhile, the U.S. Supreme Court sits enjoying their Saturday morning coffee while the nation twists in the wind.

I was angry. I was angry at Florida and I was angry with the U.S. Supreme Court in which I had so much faith. Justice Kennedy had been sitting on Bush's request for an injunction for almost a full day. Time was running out and the fraudulent vote count was about to get underway. In some Florida counties, the count was progressing while other still had no idea and couldn't agree on which votes to count and how to count them.

Noon PST

As we fiddled around the house with Alexis and Ryan, a bulletin came screaming off the television. The U.S. Supreme Court had issued a stay and ordered a halt to all manual recounts in Florida pending a hearing in front of them on Monday, December 11.

"Holy crap," I said to Eliete.

"Maybe this time they'll get it right," Eliete said

"I don't think Kennedy would have stopped the counts unless he had the votes to stop it all together for good. Man, this is what I've been waiting for. They better do what's right," I said.

The fact Kennedy had stopped the counting was a crushing blow to Gore. As I will explore later, the decision of the Supreme Court of the United States to at least temporarily stop the counting in Florida signified the end. No matter what the Supreme Court had ruled, time was ticking away and Gore couldn't afford to lose and hour let a lone two days.

I remember thinking to myself that the Supreme Court might let us down again. After all, the first time they had a crack at it they deferred to the nut jobs in Florida. But there was a sense the court would act with resolution this time to put an end to the stalemate one way or another. I'd be lying if I said I didn't want Bush to prevail but I also wanted the election to end period.

One thing was certain, we were reaching the end of the national embarrassment and I was all for that.

FIFTEEN

Days of Reckoning

December 11

After working overtime and burning the proverbial Midnight oil, lawyers for both sides submitted their briefs to the U.S. Supreme Court arguing their case and hoping for a victory. The cases were really nothing more than what both attorneys had argued in front of the court before.

Holding true to his ego's call, David Boies replaced Laurence Tribe as the lead attorney and would present the case before the Supremes. Boies had to convince the court the recounts must continue in order to discern the will of the voters. While Boies argument was difficult, it was clear he had justices that were swaying his way. I won't go into background of each Justice, you can do that on your own and thank me later. But Justices Ginsberg, Souter, Breyer and even Kennedy all seemed to be sliding Gore's way. But Boies had the tide coming against him. There was no doubt now that time had really run out and whatever the Supreme Court decided would surely put an end to the extended election.

For the Bush team, again Ted Olson was again in front of the court to prove to them he had a federal issue they must address. Olson's case was to convince really one Justice, that being Sandra Day O'Connor, that not only was Bush's Constitutional rights violated with the continued manual recounts in Florida, but that also the Florida Supreme Court acted in jest by continuing to extend the deadline and thereby violating federal law.

Noon PST

The arguments in front of the Supreme Court were a long stretch of agonizing hours for me. The long election, the constant ebb and flow of highlights and lowlights, was about to come to an end.

I was in my first day of work at my new job at Intuit Inc., one of America's top software companies. It was a day of orientation and I was very excited about my new professional direction. But my mind also kept wandering back to what was happening on the banks of the Potomac River. I had plenty on my mind; did I make the right job choice? Would I succeed? Would the people I now work with respect and like me? Would the Supreme Court rule for Bush?

I remember wanting so badly to get through the orientation to get to my new desk and check the Internet for any news on the pending case. I knew there wouldn't be a decision that day but I wanted to get the latest blow-by-blow. To me I felt I could discern what the court would do based on the line of questioning by the justices, and mostly O'Connor. The vote would hinge on her decision and I felt pretty good about the fact she would go for what was right.

I quickly ate lunch, got to my desk, and it was Yahoo time.

Click the browser.

Check the latest headlines from Associated Press.

No big news.

The Florida Legislature committee charged with perhaps electing a separate slate of electors moves quickly and by a 5-2 vote decides to pass a resolution that will lead to a pro-Bush slate of electors should the U.S. Supreme Court not rule on the Constitutionality of the Florida court's action.

This insurance policy creates an uproar with Democrats all over the nation.

I felt somewhat comfortable knowing Bush had a fallback plan but even this action made me nervous. I believed in my heart and mind that Bush had won fair and square. But to have to be swept to the White House via a battle in the Congress was not a good thing for the nation.

I like to think if it was to come to the Florida Legislature naming its own electors, Bush would have backed out for the nation. Gore refused to do the same thing but I truly believed Bush, against his advisors wishes, would have fallen on his sword so the nation could move on. I believe he is a much honorable man than most people give him credit for.

One thing was for certain, should the Supreme Court go Al Gore's way, a long and protracted battle in Congress could happen. Not to mention, Al Gore could have the swing vote in the Senate thereby electing himself President of the United States.

What a mess.

5:43 p.m. PST
There is nothing in the world quite like walking in the door after a long day at work and having your child run to you as

though you've just saved the world. The smile on Alexis' face reminded how fortunate I was to be a father.

As her 30-pound body rushed toward me with arms outstretched, I felt like the luckiest man in America. It was a good day. I loved my new job and I had a great family. For those few moments after I walked out of the cold and into the warmth only a family can provide I forgot about the turmoil outside. No Gore. No Bush. No Supreme Court. Just that million-dollar smile.

I kissed my wife and then it was time for dinner. Not chicken tonight but another dish. The news flipped on, Bill O'Reilly. The guy is flat-out good.

No one really had gauged which way the court would go. By most accounts, O'Connor was leaning the Republican way and that made me feel good. The expectation was the court could decide as early as that evening. But most people agreed it probably would be one to two days before they would hand down their decision. I figured the longer they went, the worse for Bush.

The question around the dinner table that night was this: would the Supreme Court punt again?

"They have to come back for Bush," I said to Eliete.

"Bush? There's no bush," Alexis said. She didn't know what was happening around here. Politics to a 3 year old is lobbying for that extra cookie after dinner.

"Who knows. I think O'Connor will go for Bush. But guessing anymore is crazy," Eliete said.

We continued to watch the coverage. About two weeks earlier, we had written off any other network besides Fox News Channel. For both Eliete and I, the stark reality of a press completely slanted toward the Democratic point of view made us ill. It was so bad, I am devoting a later chapter to it. Heck, if I had the time, I'd write a separate book about it. Let me end this paragraph by saying I now regard Brokaw, Jennings and Rather along the same lines as a hooker. Men I used to respect had now become more like the alcoholic uncle you'd like to lock away in a back room.

Before I went off to bed, I scanned the Internet again for the latest news. One of my surprises during the whole election fiasco was the stunning silence of Matt Drudge.

The bulldog of real journalism was a personal hero. Drudge burst onto the national scene thanks to the Clinton-Lewinsky sex scandal. Drudge was the first journalist to break the story – even though people at ABC and NBC like to claim they were first. Drudge was everything I liked about journalism. He lived by the principals all journalists should live by. The guy is great; it's that simple.

But during the 2000 election, I would visit the Drudge Report at least a dozen times per day. He wasn't up to much and somewhere I like to believe it was because he was a stunned as the rest of us.

On this night, Drudge had some solid stuff about the day's activities. After reading Drudge, and turning off the computer, I had a good feeling. The Supreme Court wouldn't let us down. I knew it.

I prayed and went sleep.

December 12

The day broke with an unassuming sun. The list broke through the blinds of my bedroom reminding me I couldn't stay in the warm confines of my bed for much longer. I always have a sense of sadness and optimism when I have to get out of bed in the morning. There's something so secure about sleeping in the warm sheets of your own bed next to your spouse. You're completely secure and nothing in the world seems to matter.

6:06 a.m. PST

I turned on the shower, disrobed and climbed in.

As the warm water slapped my skin, I thought about the possibility of Bush finally prevailing and becoming the 43rd President of the United States. As the shampoo dribbled down my back, I let out a sigh and spoke out loud despite not having an audience.

"Please God, let Bush win."

At that seemingly unimportant moment in my life, the whole reason I had become so emotionally and intellectually involved in this grudge match for the White House. The moral decay of our country, the crumbling of the American family, the stranglehold of fringe political action group, the lack of a true tax break for the middle class all flooded through my mind as though I opened it for its own reality shower.

That paragraph itself is remarkable to me. As a young college student, my thoughts were much different. I hadn't given any thought to morals and ethics as it related to the governing of our nation. I was concentrating on getting through college as fast as I could while having as much fun as possible. Parties, beer, girls and all of the other things we lust after as young men. Those were the important things to me then.

Now, a father, I had come full circle and was living the life I used to say I would never lead. I think if it was

1990 and I met my current self on the street, I wouldn't like me. I would have thought I was way too conservative and unable to find compassion. Racial equality, spreading the wealth, making housing affordable – those were my hot buttons in 1990.

The truth was I still believed in everything I believed in 10 years earlier but had a better sense of reality. When you're young, and idealistic, things are so amplified. The littlest things become world issues and you live and die by what happens. When you get a little older, and have a better center about you, those things shift and priorities change. Some might say you give in to conformity or "sell out." I don't think so. I think you learn in life what really is important and then start worrying about just the basics.

After I had written the Gulbransen Manifesto in my mind while soaping up and rinsing, I climbed out of the shower, shaved, got dressed and kissed everyone goodbye. It was time to make a living, even though my mind was in D.C.

2:30 p.m. PST

As I checked Yahoo! news again, nothing. No decision had come down and no one dare guess what the Supreme Court was up to. The only facts dribbling out of the offices of the

Supreme Court was that the Justices all worked late, as did their clerks. The all arrived early the next morning and were hard at work despite the time being 5:30 p.m. EST. "What the hell is taking so long," I blurted out loud as I sat in my office.

You would have thought I would have developed some patience during this ordeal. In fact, it was the contrary. I check news sites about every five minutes waiting for the glimmer of sunshine I had hoped to see for the past year. My thoughts constantly shifted from my work back to my young family and then back to work again. I found it strange that I could concentrate on my work and be as efficient as I was.

I've given the reasons why I had so much invested in the election. I wasn't just a Clinton hater. I actually felt this was a major turning point in our nation's history Clinton had decimated our military and that made us vulnerable on a global scale. With a new son, that last thing I wanted was our nation in a position where 10-20 years down the road having to fight a major war. Clinton's buddy-buddy relationship with China scared me and it was for reasons like that I wanted him and Gore of the American stage. Our economy was soaring but the economy is not the be-all end-all as it relates to leading the United States.

I just wanted it over. A Republican president meant a stronger military and another reason Americans could have pride in their nation again. Throughout Clinton's administration, the American people were never given anything to feel proud about. It was a selfish time.

5:49 p.m. PST

As I walked through the door at home, I was again greeted by Alexis with a hug and a kiss. I swept her off her feet and raced for the television. I had been listening to news radio during my commute home but the coverage was sporadic at best. Eliete was already watching Fox News Channel and I asked the inevitable question.

"Any news yet? Did they say there's a decision coming?"

"Not yet. They did say the Justices and clerks are still there so it might happen tonight," Eliete said. She quickly moved to give me a peck on the cheek and then onto the kitchen to finish dinner.

"Man, I hope the finish this tonight. I don't think my brain can take anymore of this up and down stuff. If they send it back to Florida I am going to lose it. I'm telling you; get ready to move to Italy. I can find work doing anything, I don't care," I said on a long run of thoughts.

"You don't speak Italian," Eliete said.

"So. I can learn. I don't care. I'm not afraid of poverty as long as I can feed you guys," I said.

My wife just smiled and turned her attention to my daughter who was gain lobbying for some sort of sweet.

7:00 p.m. PST

Eliete and I were busy folding laundry on our bed as our two children milled around in their bedroom watching cartoons and playing. Ryan was only a week old but he often sat with his sister just wondering what was going on in this new big world he found himself in.

As I turned my attention away from the TV to talk to my wife, I heard a panicked sense of urgency in the reporter's voice. It was someone on Fox News Channel, it happened so fast I don't remember who, announcing the Court had issued an opinion and that a producer was on his way to deliver the document to the reporter.

"Oh my God," I said. "They've got the decision."

My wife and I immediately ceased our chores and sat together to hear the word. The reporters scrambled to first get the decision and then to pour through it enough to tell all of us at home what it said.

The first words I heard were: "sent back to Florida", "remanded" and "5-4 decision."

My emotions were electrifying. At one time, anger, frustration, hate, desperation, disgust, sadness and disenfranchisement all filled my head to the point of combustion. They were sending the case back to Florida *again*. Never in my life had I experienced a more disappointing moment than when I heard the original account of the decision I seemed to be enveloped in a shell of anger and despair. I didn't hear my wife, kids or the television. In my head I felt as though I had been raped by the very system I had believed so religiously in. I was truly speechless.

After the tingling had stopped and I could feel my body again, I hugged my wife and immediately became a ball of negativity.

"It's over Elie. Our Constitution no longer means anything. This is the beginning of the end," I said in my best apocalyptic tone.

Eliete didn't offer any rebuttal. She too was disappointed and had no idea what would happen to our great nation. I could see it in her face.

I went to my daughter's room and gave her a big hug and a kiss telling her how much I loved her. She had no idea what was happening around her and that was for the best. Then it was back to the TV and the Internet to read the opinion.

It soon became clear that what the Supreme Court had done was, in essence, to issue a timeline to Gore's attorneys and the State of Florida that was impossible to make. After the reporters got through the entire document, the tone had changed. I no longer was disappointed. It was clearly a Bush victory and that would mean the end for Al Gore.

After reading the decision online, I stood and raised my arms in the air. I felt as though I had just finished a marathon and was raising my arms in victory. It felt as I had won and the victory was something I needed to savor for a few minutes. All of my negative and almost violent emotions had subsided and joy filled my heart.

The Supreme Court, in a closely argued 5-4 decision, stopped the counting for good. It all but assured a Bush victory and a Gore concession speech. Within 15 minutes of the announcement, Democratic Party Chairman Ed Rendel called on Gore to concede. It was such a drastic call for Gore to quit from a man who had been one of the staunchest Gore supporters. It felt good to see Gore's people now turn on him. I know that sounds cruel on my part but I was tired.

9:43 p.m. PST

As the pendants all agreed it was time for Gore to bow out, no word had come from the man himself. Bill Daley released a very short statement that said Gore would "sleep on it" and discuss his options with his family. It was an attempt to put on a face of respectability at a time Gore was reeling. It was good public relations move but he should have done it the same evening. Yes, it was late on the east coast but the whole nation was in a state of uncertainty. In the end, Gore's desire to run again for President in 2004 probably had something to do with his waiting. He needed to craft a good speech so as he departed the American political scene, albeit temporarily, people would remember him.

What I remember about that night was going to sleep with a big smile on my face. I thanked God, kissed my wife good night and fell asleep thinking America was in much better hands.

SIXTEEN
The Healing Begins

December 13

5:55 p.m.

The nation was waiting. It was official; Al Gore was to concede the closest Presidential race in history in just under five minutes. The word had come down earlier in the day and Gore, much like his mentor Bill Clinton, wanted to bow out on national television during prime time. The Clinton administration had used television so well and Gore was about to speak in front of the very same cameras he usually found no comfort in.

I made sure I was home early enough to watch the speech. The biggest question on most American's minds was whether Gore would take any parting shots on his way out the door. Would he question Bush's legitimacy? Would he mention the Florida vote again?

6:00 p.m. PST

As Gore strolled to the microphone, I couldn't help but feel sorry for him. I felt sorry because I could feel his pain. We've all lost at something we so wanted to win and Gore was about to see his lifelong dream end. His speech began and I couldn't help but swallow the lump now in my throat. Here is his speech:

Good evening.

Just moments ago, I spoke with George W. Bush and congratulated him on becoming the 43rd president of the United States, and I promised him that I wouldn't call him back this time.

I offered to meet with him as soon as possible so that we can start to heal the divisions of the campaign and the contest through which we just passed.

Almost a century and a half ago, Senator Stephen Douglas told Abraham Lincoln, who had just defeated him for the presidency, "Partisan feeling must yield to patriotism. I'm with you, Mr. President, and God bless you."

Well, in that same spirit, I say to President-elect Bush that what remains of partisan rancor must now be put aside, and may God bless his stewardship of this country.

Neither he nor I anticipated this long and difficult road. Certainly neither of us wanted it to happen. Yet it came, and now it has ended, resolved, as it must be resolved, through the honored institutions of our democracy.

Over the library of one of our great law schools is inscribed the motto, "Not under man but under God and law." That's the ruling principle of American freedom, the source of our democratic liberties. I've tried to make it my guide throughout this contest as it has guided America's deliberations of all the complex issues of the past five weeks.

Now the U.S. Supreme Court has spoken. Let there be no doubt, while I strongly disagree with the court's decision, I accept it. I accept the finality of this outcome, which will be ratified next Monday in the Electoral College. And tonight, for the sake of our unity of the people and the strength of our democracy, I offer my concession.

I also accept my responsibility, which I will discharge unconditionally, to honor the new president elect and do everything possible to help him bring Americans together in fulfillment of the great vision that our Declaration of Independence defines and that our Constitution affirms and defends.

Let me say how grateful I am to all those who supported me and supported the cause for which we have fought. Tipper and I feel a deep gratitude to Joe and Hadassah Lieberman who brought passion and high purpose to our partnership and opened new doors, not just for our campaign but for our country.

This has been an extraordinary election. But in one of God's unforeseen paths, this belatedly broken impasse can point us all to a new common ground, for its very closeness can serve to remind us that we are one people with a shared history and a shared destiny.

Indeed, that history gives us many examples of contests as hotly debated, as fiercely fought, with their own challenges to the popular will.

Other disputes have dragged on for weeks before reaching resolution. And each time, both the victor and the vanquished have accepted the result peacefully and in the spirit of reconciliation.

So let it be with us.

I know that many of my supporters are disappointed. I am too. But our disappointment must be overcome by our love of country.

And I say to our fellow members of the world community, let no one see this contest as a sign of American weakness. The strength of American democracy is shown most clearly through the difficulties it can overcome.

Some have expressed concern that the unusual nature of this election might hamper the next president in the conduct of his office. I do not believe it need be so.

President-elect Bush inherits a nation whose citizens will be ready to assist him in the conduct of his large responsibilities.

I personally will be at his disposal, and I call on all Americans — I particularly urge all who stood with us to unite behind our next president. This is America. Just as we fight hard when the stakes are high, we close ranks and come together when the contest is done.

And while there will be time enough to debate our continuing differences, now is the time to recognize that that which unites us is greater than that which divides us.

While we yet hold and do not yield our opposing beliefs, there is a higher duty than the one we owe to political party. This is America and we put country before party. We will stand together behind our new president.

As for what I'll do next, I don't know the answer to that one yet. Like many of you, I'm looking forward to spending the holidays with family and old friends. I know I'll spend time in Tennessee and mend some fences, literally and figuratively.

Some have asked whether I have any regrets and I do have one regret: that I didn't get the chance to stay and fight for the American people over the next four years, especially for those who need burdens lifted and barriers removed, especially for those who feel their voices have not been heard. I heard you and I will not forget.

I've seen America in this campaign and I like what I see. It's worth fighting for and that's a fight I'll never stop.

As for the battle that ends tonight, I do believe as my father once said, that no matter how hard the loss, defeat might serve as well as victory to shape the soul and let the glory out.

So for me this campaign ends as it began: with the love of Tipper and our family; with faith in God and in the country I have been so proud to serve, from Vietnam to the vice presidency; and with gratitude to our truly tireless campaign staff and volunteers, including all those who worked so hard in Florida for the last 36 days.

Now the political struggle is over and we turn again to the unending struggle for the common good of all Americans and for those multitudes around the world that look to us for leadership in the cause of freedom.

In the words of our great hymn, "America, America": "Let us crown thy good with brotherhood, from sea to shining sea."

And now, my friends, in a phrase I once addressed to others, it's time for me to go.

Thank you and good night, and God bless America.

I was shocked. Gore's speech was delivered with such passion and conviction, I found myself connected to this robot of a man. I had to admit to myself that if this Al Gore had run for president, being humble and full of personality, the contest wouldn't have been close. As much as I believed in Bush, Gore's speech was phenomenal. And although I was glad to finally see him give in, I respected his words and his feelings. He let us into his heart for the first time and it was touching.

The speech, given an hour before Bush would give his victory speech, was the official end of the election. I felt good about that. I felt bad for Al Gore. Somewhere I hoped he realized by being himself he touched more people than he had ever before. As scary as it may seem, I thought if he could capture that sentiment and block out the special interests and staffers, he may have another good shot at winning. But Gore would not run again. Instead, he endorsed crack-pot Howard Dean in 2004.

7:00 p.m. PST

The networks had devoted their last half-hour to discussing what Bush must do in his acceptance speech to start the healing of America. Certainly the nation was evenly divided. Bush had lost the popular vote and carried the Electoral College by the slimmest margin ever. Many in the media made so much ado bout his speech, you would have figured he was still running for office. In many ways, he was.

Bush decided to give his speech from the State House in Austin, Texas. The idea was to drive home the image that Bush was a unifying force, not a dividing one. Bush had won the accolades of Democrats in the House of Texas after working through partisanship to really accomplish good things in Austin. This setting, it was thought, would be an example of how Bush would lead as president. It was a good idea but no one really knew if it would help the healing.

The more liberal media members all put tremendous pressure on Bush to deliver a stunning speech. Gore, who an hour earlier had give his speech, had set a high bar for Bush. In reality, America, founded by underdogs itself, would never rate the speeches on the same level. We felt sorry for Gore and we're a compassionate people.

Bush entered the State House with his wife Laura to rousing applause. Looking as though the heaviest of weights had been lifted from his shoulders, a rejuvenate Bush waved and began to speak as the audience clapped:

Thank you very much. Thank you.

Thank you very much. Good evening, my fellow Americans. I appreciate so very much the opportunity to speak with you tonight.

Mr. Speaker, Lieutenant Governor, friends, distinguished guests, and our country has been through a long and trying period, with the outcome of the presidential election not finalized for longer than any of us could ever imagine.

Vice President Gore and I put our hearts and hopes into our campaigns. We both gave it our all. We shared similar emotions, so I understand how difficult this moment must be for Vice President Gore and his family.

He has a distinguished record of service to our country as a congressman, a senator and a vice president.

This evening I received a gracious call from the vice president. We agreed to meet early next week in Washington and we agreed to do our best to heal our country after this hard-fought contest.

Tonight I want to thank all the thousands of volunteers and campaign workers who worked so hard on my behalf.

I also salute the vice president and his supports for waging a spirited campaign. And I thank him for a call that I know was difficult to make. Laura and I wish the vice president and Senator Lieberman and their families the very best.

I have a lot to be thankful for tonight. I'm thankful for America and thankful that we were able to resolve our electoral differences in a peaceful way.

I'm thankful to the American people for the great privilege of being able to serve as your next president.

I want to thank my wife and our daughters for their love. Laura's active involvement as first lady has made Texas a better place, and she will be a wonderful first lady of America.

I am proud to have Dick Cheney by my side, and America will be proud to have him as our next vice president.

Tonight I chose to speak from the chamber of the Texas House of Representatives because it has been a home to bipartisan cooperation. Here in a place where Democrats have the majority, Republicans and Democrats have worked together to do what is right for the people we represent.

We've had spirited disagreements. And in the end, we found constructive consensus. It is an experience I will always carry with me, an example I will always follow.

I want to thank my friend, House Speaker Pete Laney, a Democrat, who introduced me today. I want to thank the legislators from both political parties with whom I've worked.

Across the hall in our Texas capitol is the state Senate. And I cannot help but think of our mutual friend, the former Democrat lieutenant governor, Bob Bullock. His love for Texas and his ability to work in a bipartisan way continue to be a model for all of us.

The spirit of cooperation I have seen in this hall is what is needed in Washington, D.C. It is the challenge of our moment. After a difficult election, we must put politics behind us and work together to make the promise of America available for every one of our citizens.

I am optimistic that we can change the tone in Washington, D.C.

I believe things happen for a reason, and I hope the long wait of the last five weeks will heighten a desire to move beyond the bitterness and partisanship of the recent past.

Our nation must rise above a house divided. Americans share hopes and goals and values far more important than any political disagreements.

Republicans want the best for our nation, and so do Democrats. Our votes may differ, but not our hopes.

I know America wants reconciliation and unity. I know Americans want progress. And we must seize this moment and deliver.

Together, guided by a spirit of common sense, common courtesy and common goals, we can unite and inspire the American citizens.

Together, we will work to make all our public schools excellent, teaching every student of every background and every accent, so that no child is left behind.

Together we will save Social Security and renew its promise of a secure retirement for generations to come.

Together we will strengthen Medicare and offer prescription drug coverage to all of our seniors.

Together we will give Americans the broad, fair and fiscally responsible tax relief they deserve.

Together we'll have a bipartisan foreign policy true to our values and true to our friends, and we will have a military equal to every challenge and superior to every adversary.

Together we will address some of society's deepest problems one person at a time, by encouraging and empowering the good hearts and good works of the American people.

This is the essence of compassionate conservatism and it will be a foundation of my administration.

These priorities are not merely Republican concerns or Democratic concerns; they are American responsibilities.

During the fall campaign, we differed about the details of these proposals, but there was remarkable consensus about the important issues before us: excellent schools, retirement and health security, tax relief, a strong military, and a more civil society.

We have discussed our differences. Now it is time to find common ground and build consensus to make America a beacon of opportunity in the 21st century.

I'm optimistic this can happen. Our future demands it and our history proves it. Two hundred years ago, in the election of 1800, America faced another close presidential election. A tie in the Electoral College put the outcome into the hands of Congress.

After six days of voting and 36 ballots, the House of Representatives elected Thomas Jefferson the third president of the United States. That election brought the first transfer of power from one party to another in our new democracy.

Shortly after the election, Jefferson, in a letter titled "Reconciliation and Reform," wrote this. "The steady character of our countrymen is a rock to which we may safely moor; unequivocal in principle, reasonable in manner. We should be able to hope to do a great deal of good to the cause of freedom and harmony."

Two hundred years have only strengthened the steady character of America. And so as we begin the work of healing our nation, tonight I call upon that character: respect for each other, respect for our differences, generosity of spirit, and a willingness to work hard and work together to solve any problem.

I have something else to ask you, to ask every American. I ask for you to pray for this great nation. I ask for your prayers for leaders from both parties. I thank you for your prayers for me and my family, and I ask you to pray for Vice President Gore and his family.

I have faith that with God's help we as a nation will move forward together as one nation, indivisible. And together we will create and America that is open, so every citizen has access to the American dream; an America that is educated, so every child has the keys to realize that dream; and an America that is united in our diversity and our shared American values that are larger than race or party.

I was not elected to serve one party, but to serve one nation.

The president of the United States is the president of every single American, of every race and every background.

Whether you voted for me or not, I will do my best to serve your interests and I will work to earn your respect.

I will be guided by President Jefferson's sense of purpose, to stand for principle, to be reasonable in manner, and above all, to do great good for the cause of freedom and harmony.

The presidency is more than an honor. It is more than an office. It is a charge to keep, and I will give it my all.

Thank you very much and God bless America.

I felt Bush's speech was extremely effective. Was it as moving as Gore's, no. But it didn't need to be. Bush wasn't saying goodbye; he was saying hello. He referred to the work he did with State senators in Texas and that sent a clear signal he would work to get through partisan politics to deliver on his campaign promises and deliver to the American people. It was a long speech sometimes reiterating policy points he made during the campaign but he wanted to, again, remind Americans what is beliefs were.

I print these speeches in this book because I believe it's important to understand how this election ended. It ended with half of the nation bitterly disappointed and the other half elated. Bush had received more popular votes in the 2000 election than Bill Clinton did in both of his elections and he won by a landslide. As Bush spoke, many talked about his lack of a mandate by the people because he hadn't won the popular vote. In reality, Bush had a mandate stronger than any president since Ronald Reagan and his speech was the first step in rescuing the moral fiber of the United States.

10:09 p.m.

It was now officially over and I wondered what I would do with all the time I now had freed up with the election still a fresh and stale memory in my mind. I checked in on the kids and realized what I could do with that time.

I had been keeping a journal throughout the election because I felt it important to describe to Alexis and Ryan what happened during those insane 36 days. As I watched them sleep, I wondered if they would even read it. I wondered if I should put it away in a box and open it when they were old enough to understand or if I should include it with my own belongings to be opened in their later years and after I had passed on.

To me, and maybe it was because I had watched too many movies, it was always romantic to hear stories of children or grandchildren stumbling across historical documents of their dead relatives. These documents offered a rare and intimate look at history through the perspective of someone they knew and loved. A living history spoken and expressed by someone they loved made history so meaningful. It's the same when you hear your parents tell a story about the days when they grew up. They lived through things you can only read about.

So, in just one brief moment, looking at the silhouettes of my two children, I decided to take my journal and make it into full ‑blown book. I had been working on two fictional novels at the time the whole election mess came about and they had been on hold. My extra time was filled with watching every detail of what was happening in Florida. As I shut their door and went to bed with my grand idea, it felt good to be American again. But I also thought of those passionate Democrats who must have felt like they were slugged in the gut. Although I disagreed with their policies and practices, my thoughts went out to them hoping we could all work together as citizens to start to heal.

After Thoughts

SEVENTEEN

It's About the Dialogue

The presidential election of 2000 came to an end after 36 days when a collective nation fought for their beliefs. During the political season, it's easy to chose sides and support the candidate we personally believe in. I wanted Bush and I contributed both money and time to his campaign to do my part to help America go in the direction I felt it should go. Although not everyone shared my opinions, I was happy to see so many take a more active role in the political process despite a continuation in low voter turnout and widespread voter apathy.

I shared with you the first reason I penned this book - as a written historical record of my views and experiences during the most contested presidential election in U.S. history. But I also had another reason. That reason, even though it might sound self-serving and somewhat righteous, was to share with other Americans my thoughts so they could better understand my reasoning and desire for a fundamental change in American government.

Being a conservative these days in America is almost as bad as being a Nazi during World War II. Everyone equates the title "conservative" with bigotry, wealth, the pro-life movement, fundamental Christianity and gay bashing. In a nation with a beautiful system designed around the exchange of free thought and free speech, labeling anyone anything is not fair.

I have used plenty of labels in this book: liberals, Democrats, etc. I used those as descriptions more than I use them to judge someone's character or intent.
The election of 2000 for me was a coming out party. I wanted to tell the world I was conservative and I don't feel bad about it. I can say that because I don't have hate in my heart for anyone. I don't hate minorities (I married one!), I don't hate gays, I don't hate pro-choice or pro-life supporters and I don't hate Democrats. I may disagree with them on the issues but that doesn't mean I lack compassion and understanding when it comes to the issues they hold important in their own hearts.

When Bill Clinton was elected to office in 1992, I didn't vote for him. I didn't vote for George H.W. Bush either. I vote my conscience at the time and unfortunately that conscience told me to vote for Ross Perot. I was turned off by both political parties at that time in my life so I went against my own party. I then switched my party affiliation.

But I had a sense America was changing. I looked around me at the violence, drug abuse, poverty and other social issues and came to the realization that all the problems started in the home. Sure, drug use doesn't happen because kids don't get love from their parents. Some of the most heavy drug users come from wealthy, balanced families. When I look at the problems facing our society I realize we are turning outward looking for problems instead of looking in the mirror. The age of "Personal Irresponsibility" as I call it. We're living in a time when many people refuse to take responsibility for their own actions. Parent refuse to be held responsible for their kids actions, they refuse to hold their own children accountable for their missteps in life. That is dangerous and it's being perpetuated by certain segments of our society.

I was tired of this moving into 2000. I had a family complete with children and I looked at the world in a much different way than I did at age 22. It wasn't about me or my generation anymore instead giving way to what I would leave behind for my children and grandchildren. This crusade I am on includes this book. I want people who agree and disagree to read it and give me passionate feedback. I am for working toward a common goal. A common goal that includes saving the family and the children we bring into this world each day.

Even other conservatives may read this and disagree and that is a good thing. We need to create a dialogue about these issues instead of whispering in hushed tones afraid we might be branded a "racist" or "gay basher." The time for name calling has come and gone.

The next few chapters include my opinion on the people, places and issues that made up the 2000 Election. I hope in reading these opinions you'll find your own view whether you agree with me or not.

EIGHTEEN
The Hangover

So what did we exactly learn from this harrowing experience? The answer is probably more individual in nature than most might think. While the scholarly historians take the next 10 years evaluating what lasting effect the election of 2000 had on our collective nation, for most Americans the results are something we live each day.

The election screamed that we were a nation divided almost perfectly equal with two sides swiftly moving apart.

The left wanted to continue the pursuits of the past eight years under the Clinton administration pushing more government involvement in our lives while the right pushed for traditional values and a "hands off" approach with the federal government. Both sides were as equally passionate about what direction they felt the country should travel. In times past, the differences have never been so great. It explains the lack of cooperation we've seen and continue to see. This puts an excessive amount of strain on government who can't seem to get through even the most benign chores associated with governing.

In my opinion, when you break it done to the bare bones of what is dividing us, it's really rather simple. For the most part, half of Americans see the move away from a more traditional values and morals as a positive outcome of a rapidly evolving nation. The progress made over the past 30 years related to technology and healthcare have resulted in the best economy since the end of World War II coupled with a longer life expectancy for most Americans. Due to those strides, we face higher populations who need and desire services; some of them currently provided by the federal government.

Democrats in general consider most important issues related to the social ills of our democratic society. The rise in the homeless population in the late 1980s and the continued environmental problems we see all over the globe are at the forefront of many American's political agendas. Civil rights is another key issue to Democrats who have expanded their desire to make sure every American is allowed to pursue their dream without the threat of bigotry of discrimination. Today, civil rights organizations fight just as hard for disabled Americans as they did for Blacks in the 1960s. They fight for gay rights including the right of "domestic partners" to be eligible for health benefits from employers.

I would not argue with one point the Democrats make on their agenda nor would I say their intention is not honorable, and at it's base, patriotic. Americans have always opened their arms to those less fortunate or to those being persecuted. And, despite the gains made over the past 40 years, there still remains a serious racial and economic division between the "haves" and "have-nots" in this country.

But, just as the Republicans struggled with a rogue faction controlling their part in the early 1990s, the Democrats have also been overrun with ultra liberals who also believe in the valid social issues listed about but also despise anyone who does not agree with them enough to practice the ritual of personal destruction. The Clinton White House was the breeding ground for this and its hate mongering tactics can only be described as bullying and strong-armed. The Democratic Party lost much of its compassionate feel and gained a hard edge that drove more conservative voters like me away. I may believe we should help the homeless but I also believe in God and an American's right to exercise their opinion – not matter if it agrees with popular sentiment or not. And in today's heavily Democratic America, if you speak out, you're branded a bigot or an outcast. That hardly screams compassion to me.

But Democrats, for the most part seem to be content with where our society is heading. They don't seem bothered as much about the changing American family and the lack of a cohesive religious community. The approach is more logical; not based on religious conviction or moral guidelines. Today's Democrat seems to be saying "Do whatever makes you happy as long as it doesn't break the law or hurt anyone." On the surface, that doesn't sound half bad.

Conservatives relished the opportunity to "take America back" during the 2000 election. Due to Clinton's infidelities and seemingly endless ethical gaffes, half of the nation wanted to take a step back and return to the days when religion was stronger and we spent more time together as families and pushed agendas aimed at helping everyone attain the American dream.

What's laughable to me is the conclusion most Democrats take when the label Republicans as conservatives. They immediately draw a picture of white, wealthy Americans who care nothing about their fellow human beings. An evil group bent on shoving religion down the throat of Americans the point we return to the early days of America when Puritanism ruled the day. It's an age where old fashioned is another term for prude.

But for us conservatives brave (or stupid!) enough to stand up and tell what we believe, this was perhaps one last opportunity to return faith and dignity to government and particularly the White House. Clinton literally and figuratively stained the office and Republicans felt it was their duty to undo the excesses of the 90s under Clinton.

I may be speaking for myself but I know many of my fellow conservative Republicans feel our society is beginning to spin out of control. The nation in which we were raised seems to be a distant and faded memory. No longer can our children roam the neighborhoods growing their imagination instead of obsessing about being abducted or killed in their neighborhoods and schools. This loss of innocence is one of my primary drivers to conservative thought. I don't presume every American should practice the same religion that I do but religion does teach our children respect, morals and gives them a roadmap that doesn't lead to destruction.

We've smashed our moral compass and we need to look to faith as a way to bring us through our complex modern problem. These problems are not always easily answered by human beings so what do you do? Many people have just given up. They kill themselves and others acting out of rage and frustration. These incidents have increased in recent years and many don't acknowledge the problem. They think by just moving on the problem will go away but they're wrong.

The causes of problems like drug addiction, teenage sex and violence are not the creation of Democrats and their style of governing. It would be foolish and irresponsible to claim such a thing.

Then again, President Clinton admits to smoking marijuana as a teenager (as I did) and to receiving oral sex in the Oval Office despite being a married man. How can we in good faith tell our children not to do these things when the leader of our own nation admits it. It gives a sense of approval that is not easily measured.

Conservatives want traditional values back in place. We want kids to respect their parents and elders, we want faith to be something you celebrate instead of suppress and we want children, and the goal of protecting them, to be our top priority. These were the issues for us in 2000. We wanted to go back to the time of Ronald Regan when we could be proud of America and all that it stood for. We want to be proud of our leader and be able to look our children in the eye and tell them they are role models.

In George W. Bush, we saw our knight in shining armor. We saw a man who bridged the passionate conservatives of the present and future with the traditional conservatives of the past. Bush was our bridge to Reagan and a man we all believed could lead us back to where we came from.

NINETEEN
The Fork in the Road

Here we are. Which way will we go? Who will lead us and what will this path lead us to?

These are the questions that faced American voters on November 7, 2000. They clearly had to choose which direction, and which man, would lead the nation into an exciting new century. Would we continue the Clinton/Gore path or would be choose to ride Bush to a new frontier? That was the question and what did Americans say?

They couldn't decide. To even think the election would come down to under 1,000 votes would make anyone laugh before it actually happened. But it did happen and it sent a major warning signal to all of us that we are divided and we all know what they say about a house divided.

By the slimmest of margins, Americans handed George W. Bush to the collective car we call America and said:

"You drive. Just make sure you take the correct side of that fork in the road."

America has put its faith now in George W. Bush. Many of us fought hard to help him get there but there are 50 percent of the people who believed he shouldn't have the opportunity. So we come to a time in our nation's history that is of vital importance to us all. We must work toward a common goal and bridge the massive gap that separates one side from the other. We may never all agree 100 percent on all the issue but clearly our nation has never been so divided as we are today. It is surprising considering the enormous wealth and prosperity we are currently enjoying. In times like these, an incumbent opponent is supposed to win my huge margins due to an electorate that understands it's not good to rock the boat when things are sailing along so smoothly. But that's exactly what we did.

Because of the decisive nature in which he won the White House, many on the left would have you believe Bush has to be conciliatory and shoot to be more moderate than he would like if he expects to be successful. That assumption is wrong and if Bush expects to be successful, he'll have to instill fear in his opponents.

When Ronald Regan became the 40th President of the United States, he always had a grandfatherly appearance and demeanor about him while in public or in front of the media. He was even tame when talking with the opposition in congress. But because he was The Great Communicator, thus having the complete support of the American people, he was feared on Capital Hill. If you screwed with Ronnie, you better not go home because your constituents would blame you, not the likable president. This fear lasted for eight years and contributed to the legend that is Ronald Regan.

Bush must take this lesson and instill that same fear in Americans today. Fear is a great motivator, especially for politicians who face re-election. If Bush is to be successful, and start moving those from the left to the moderate right, he has to gain the trust of the American people in the same way Regan did.

My concern, and the reason I voted for Bush, is we may have traveled so far down one path, there might not be any room to turn around. It's not advisable for America to take the path less traveled, instead, we need to take lessons learned, slip our feet into footprints left long ago and return to the glory and honor once valued by all of America. Only then will be begin to stem the tide. And my hope is, George W. Bush is the man to do that.

TWENTY

The Donkeys

I know, I know. Calling Democrats Donkeys may seem a bit of a smart ass move. I could have used "Jack Asses" or just "Asses" but I chose the high road.

Going into November 7, 2000, I thought I had a good sense of what the Democratic Party was all about. After all, I had been a member for a few years and made a hobby out of following politics and politicians. But things had changed since Bill Clinton took office in the early 1990s. The Party had strayed away from some of the issues I found important to me. It seemed as though the stamp Clinton put on the party was so big it really overshadowed it and convoluted its issues.

The party has always been championed by the working man and woman of America. This is due in part to the strong presence of labor unions in America that have helped support the party financially and by getting the vote out with key demographic groups including blacks and other minorities. It has always been the choice of people who feel as though they are missing the American dream due to economic and racial disadvantages.

In many ways, the Democratic Party did a good job voice the concerns of everyday Americans. Throughout the 1960s it led an important civil rights movement that resulted in opportunities today not available to every American just 40 years ago.

But somehow, after the rise of the Republicans in the 1980s, the Democratic Party lost its true focus. It shifted away from the "everyman" approach and started to bow to special interest as much as any other party. No longer did labor unions hold the power they once yielded thanks to stronger federal laws aimed at protecting the American worker. Gone was the day of Jimmy Hoffa and the backroom politics of Chicago and Mayor Richard Daley, Sr.

The turning point for me was Clinton himself. He was a charming young president when he was sworn in January 21, 1993, but his motives were hardly to strengthen the party. Whatever promises he made, and to whom he made them to, superceded the needs of Democrats and their party. When Clinton made gays in the military is first issue after assuming office, he made a powerful enemy in the military and the American public was less than impressed with his policy.

I agree with gays being able to serve in the military. But Clinton's desire to make gay soldiers mainstream and to be open about their sexuality was a serious miscalculation. Anyone who has intimate knowledge of the workings of the military knows the bottom line is conformity. That's why they shave soldier's heads. First to humiliate them, next to show they are no different from anyone else. By making sexuality an issue, Clinton suddenly made a small group of soldiers stick out from the rest. That's not good for military morale and it doesn't breed acceptance, it breeds discontent.

Let me make something perfectly clear, all Americans, no matter their race, sexual preference or religious beliefs, deserves equal protection under the law and should not be discriminated against. But why single in on one small group and trumpet their differences? Should we celebrate our differences? Yes. Should we in the military? No.

Again, Clinton charged ahead with an issue unimportant to most of us. Gays comprise less than 3 percent of the total population of the United States. That doesn't mean they should be protected or represented in governing but overall the majority rules. Since when is sexual preference an issue we should discuss openly? I don't run around telling people I like women.

Sure, I'm not in a minority butI don't discuss my sexual preference one way or another. It's a personal issue. If someone is gay, fine. But does that mean you walk down the street telling everyone you meet? Some people believe that it should be the way. I do not. Your personal sexual preference should be just that - personal. What anyone does behind the doors of their own bedroom doesn't concern me and I wouldn't tell people what they should do. But yet Clinton made such a large issue of it, it ended up hurting the gay men and women serving or that wanted to serve.

I use this example not to disparage gays or their cause. I use to point on the Democrat's desire to ramrod issues that don't have broad support. This is how the Clinton Years would all be. The party took a back seat to Clinton and it never recovered. Even when the man is president, he should never overshadow the platform of the party or what the core of the party believes in. Clinton did that and the core followed not because they agreed but because Clinton was able to convince them to follow his own personal agenda. He was a remarkable politician and perhaps the best of our time.

The Democrats went into the Election of 2000 a little over confident in my book. Much like George H.W. Bush relied on the push he received from the Gulf War in 1992, Al Gore was riding the wave of America's best economy in 30 years. The dot-com craze on Wall Street mixed with almost six years of economic growth, fooled them into thinking it would be cakewalk. Bob Dole offered not challenge in 1996 and the Democrats had no real fear of George W. Bush avenging his father's loss of 8 years earlier. Bush was raising a ton of money but the good times of the 90s seemed to be enough to carry Gore to the White House despite is lack of personal charisma.

This was the largest of the Democrat's strategic mistakes in the campaign of 2000. I don't care how well you're doing or how insignificant your opponent seems, you have to always run as though you are the underdog. I don't care if you're in a football game or running for the school board, an upstart can always upset you if you don't work as though you have to make up the ground.

When the Democrats wisely detached themselves from the scandal-plagued Clinton, they made a wise move that worked to a point. Gore needed to run as his own man. The problem was, he wasn't exciting and he couldn't really motivate the party like Clinton had. His handlers tried but they really couldn't prop him up like he needed to. Now if the Gore who delivered the concession speech ran, he might have won big.

But where the Democrats really changed and chased me from their ranks was with their policy of personally destroying anyone who disagrees with them. This goes far beyond politicians and right through to our neighborhoods. If someone disagreed with any of their policies, they were targeted for a smear campaign that not only destroyed their political position but also was aimed to embarrass them personally. It didn't matter if the man or woman had kids or a spouse; just go for the jugular.

This policy came back to bite the Democrats in January 1998 when Drudge broke the Lewinsky affair. My contention is, even with the thousand and thousands of media sources now operating today, and the competition born from that, it never would have made it into the press had the Republicans not been looking to payback Clinton for all the lives he had destroyed. Many presidents, including John F. Kennedy, had mistresses on the side but those details never made it into the press until years after he was dead. Clinton had not earned that unilateral respect because Republicans were tired of being brow-beaten.

What is sad and disappointing about the new Democratic Party is the tactics they now utilize. One of my favorite Americans is Martin Luther King, Jr. Amid a swelling threat of violence and hate no one would like to be subjected to, King always held his cool and called for all of us to come together. He was a true unifying force. He didn't want special treatment or perks - he just wanted equality.

I wonder what he'd think today when Democrats are as quick to label people "bigots" or "zealots" at the drop of a hat as they did in the 1950s and 60s when the civil rights movement picked up steam. It's now a Democratic Party practicing intolerance under the guise of promoting tolerance. It fights for the rights of minority groups while making those who are not a minority feel dirty and guilty. That's not right and it's not what America is about. You shouldn't shoot for equality by shooting down others who may have enjoyed success or privilege.

Throughout the 36-day election, the Democrats again attacked like a dog fighting for its life. The Democrats devised, in advance of the election, ways to prolong it and by time to create votes. Is there proof? Sure. Can I get it? No. But that's my opinion. I truly believe, when they learned the contest may be very close, they set in motion a plan to create havoc to hold onto power. The Democrats had intelligence that spoke to the antiquated voting system in several key states. They knew if the tallies were close, they could run into action challenging the validity by creating confusion and anger. They prey on the fears of America and it has worked for eight years up until now. That's why I and so many other Americans were so angry. They were cheating but at the same time calling Republicans cheaters. It was infuriating.

In retrospect, I don't blame some people for believing the charges. After all, there are segments of the population just trying to hold on and they already feel they are at a disadvantage.

It was this fear mongering and complete lack of respect for the American people and for the ethics we all live by that made me so angry with Democrats. In many ways, it drove people back to the right. A younger population now aging and seeing the result of the past eight years. The Democratic Party was starting to loose touch and the astonishing point was they didn't see it.

TWENTY ONE

Al Gore

One of the biggest lies ever perpetrated on the American people was that Al Gore was not a man of wealth and privilege. Was he a multi-millionaire capable of sitting back and counting his money? No. But he grew up in The Beltway and he was a product of a powerful family as in touch with America's minorities as Eminem.

I found it remarkable that so many followed a man they really knew so little about. They knew the information the Gore people wanted them to know but no one seemed to dig deep. No reporter talked about Gore's black nanny and how she would have to wait in the car when Gore's father, the famous senator from Tennessee, would take the family to "white-only" restaurants. To Gore's credit, he would bring his nanny food out to the car showing that he has a good bone in his body.

When I look at Al Gore from 10,000 feet, I don't have any ill will what so ever. Instead, I have a sort of depressing like for the man. He is a complete product of his environment. His father bred him to one day be president and it has been his goal since his earliest memories of childhood. It's no different than the overzealous father who pushes their son or daughter into sports to live vicariously through there by erasing their own failures. Gore isn't to blame for who he has become. Only recently has he had the chance to stand up and be himself. Ironically, it was at the hour of his worst defeat.

Gore, raised in a suite at a hotel in Washington, D.C., lived a sheltered live of rigidity. Not until he broke free and went to Harvard did he enjoy freedom and even experimentation with marijuana. Just like all of us, he explored while a student and would pay the price during his first run for the Democratic presidential nomination in 1988. The revelation about pot use, really his only mistake of any significance in his closely monitored life, snapped him back into shape. I can hear his father telling him "I told you so."

I don't mean to make Al Gore into some tragic figure. Certainly he has a loving family and a life most of us would be lucky to live. But you cannot overlook the cautiousness of his life. Brought up in a bubble where emotion was a weakness.

It was his inability to connect to a large segment of the population that would be his undoing in the election. Gore's policies closely followed those of the previous administration along with some economic policies all his own. But he was unable to sell it in total to the American people. His stiff demeanor and catatonic tone were hard to get excited about. Many could overlook this and instead delve into his views on the issues but it wasn't exciting. He was Stan Laurel to Clinton's Oliver Hardy. He was Stephen Wright to Clinton's Andrew "Dice" Clay. They both might be talented but one overwhelmingly knocks you upside the head and makes you notice.

Gore was a human sleeping pill. You could slap "Unisom" on him and no one would notice. This lack of excitement failed to ignite the Democratic Party enough to create the landslide they felt they deserved. It was amazing that Gore won the popular vote as he did. Gore tallied 50,996,116 votes in the general election besting his opponent by 500,000 votes. This total seems amazing when you look at a map of the nation and realize Gore was trounced overall. He picked up a majority of his votes in major U.S. cities like Los Angeles, New York, Chicago, San Francisco and Boston. Numbers sometimes lie and these do as well. But it was an accomplishment. Some people liked his message but in the end, the lack of strategy and preparation by his campaign resulted in a loss when he should have clearly won.

There is a dark side to Gore I fear. Like Clinton, he suggests our nation move to a more global village model. When words like "global" or "international" are thrown around in relation to how our nation governs itself, which is scary. It is not a time to blur our borders and our sovereignty. Gore advocates the use of the United Nations to resolve our international disputes. I don't trust the UN to protect the interests of the United States. It's a body made up of countries that aspire to be like the United States while at the same time eyeing our wealth. This globalist point of view employed by Gore is a direct threat to all of us. His relations with the Chinese and willingness to continue Clinton's hands-off policy concerning China is both irresponsible and unwise. China is now our greatest threat and to be taking money for campaigns from them should raise the muster of even the strongest Democrat.

Whatever Al Gore decides to do next, there were always be a sharp split on what American's think of him. He's divisive figure on the American political landscape and no one seems to know who the real Al Gore is.

TWENTY TWO

Jesse, Jesse, Jesse!

What makes Jesse Jackson so appealing to his community?

Strides have been made for black Americans since the days of Martin Luther King, Jr. There is still a long way to go but I cannot figure why a more intelligent, educated and exciting leader hasn't emerged. Jackson, who has done some things worth credit to his character, seems to follow in the steps of his friend Al Gore.

When the recount issue hit just one day after the close presidential vote had take place, Jackson, almost beating the television camera, immediately made it a race issues stating blacks were intimidated from voting in Florida causing votes for Al Gore not to be cast or to be cast aside. He seems to flourish in confusion while molding an issue to fit his own personal and political needs. In this case, he rushed to judgment and immediately planned protests. Those initial protests were stopped by Bush supporters recognizing what Jackson was up to.

Looking into the life of Jesse Jackson, you wonder too how he can preach about poverty and racial inequality while leading a life of luxury – tax free. Jackson, who is the head of the civil rights group The Rainbow Coalition/PUSH, lives in a massive home in Chicago decked out in decorations fit for a king. He wears $5,000 suits and travels all over the world while billing everything to his non-profit group. Doesn't that smell fishy to anyone?

Jackson has no set job or income. He gains money by charging to speak but yet lives way beyond the money he makes speaking. I bring these points up not to discredit the civil rights movement, or for a need for a strong black leader to look out for their interests, but to point out how bad he is for these causes. Members of Jackson's group might not care what mainstream America thinks of them and their leader but they should. Jackson is not a good ambassador for the black people. His actions during the 2000 election, where he accused racial injustice at the polls was horrendous.

The 2000 presidential election resulted in the highest number of black Americans exercising their right to vote. In fact, according to the State of Florida, although blacks account for 13 percent of the state's population, the black vote represented 15 percent of the votes cast in 2000 in Florida. Yet Jackson never addressed these figures nor did the media. They simply dismissed them as to add rage and anger to their cause.

I've called Jackson a media whore throughout this book. The language might be harsh but that's what he is. Jesse Jackson may at times lend to the cause but for the most part, he's out for himself. It's really too bad because black Americans deserve better.

Just one day prior to George W. Bush's inauguration on January 20, 2001, Jackson was again embarrassed when details of an extramarital affair were revealed. On that day, I wrote this:

Et Tu Jesse?

The irony is truly staggering.

So-called civil rights leader Jesse Jackson admitted today he fathered a child with his mistress while serving as Bill Clinton's "spiritual advisor" during the Lewinsky sex scandal in 1998.

Oh, did I mention Jackson is still married?

In another example of his hypocritical public life, Jackson official acknowledged he was the father of a 20-month old little girl conceived and born out of wedlock. The mother is Rainbow Coalition activist Karin Stanford who Jackson hired in 1998 to run the Washington, D.C. office after being impressed with her book on foreign policy.

Obviously, he was impressed with much more than the 39-year old's opinion on foreign policy. It seems Jackson was more interested in foreign anatomy · outside of his marriage.

Jackson, himself born illegitimate, was quick to be humble and asked publicly for the forgiveness of his family and the public in general.
"This is no time for evasions, denials or alibis. I fully accept responsibility and I am truly sorry for my actions," said Jackson in a long written statement. "My wife, Jackie, and my children have been made aware of the child and it has been an extremely painful, trying and difficult time for them. I have asked God and each one of them to forgive me and I thank each of them for their grace and understanding throughout this period of tribulation. We have prayed together and through God's grace we have been reconciling."

Where was God in your thoughts Jesse when you sex with Stanford breaking your wedding vows? Where was God in the equation when you stood by Bill Clinton telling the world to forgive him for his infidelity?

You see, for Jesse Jackson, and I refuse to call him Reverend, God is a convenience to use when it suits him well. He believes in nothing he preaches. As I have written in this space before, Jackson is about Jackson and no one else.

One of the more shocking details of Jackson's illegitimate child carried and delivered by Stanford is how brazen he was about the affair. Not only did Jackson carry on with it for some time, he also walked a pregnant Stanford into the White House at the height of the Clinton-Lewinsky sex scandal and smiled for photo opportunities while "spiritually" counseling Clinton on his extra-marital affair.
Something tells me the two were comparing notes and not asking God or their wives for forgiveness.

Jackson is and always will be a media whore who pines for face time to increase his wealth and perceived power. He does not care deeply about his fellow Black Americans and has really done nothing of significance to battle racism in this nation. Some will point to the Million Man March and he should be commended for the organization of such a strong display of unity. But Jackson continues to "preach" about the ills of blacks and minorities in this country while living it up in a Chicago mansion and sleeping with a mistress on the side.

I can imagine how dejected some young black young men must feel today. In a country where over 60 percent of black children grow up with a single parent, mostly their mother, the most visible black leader in America fathers an illegitimate child. A child he will see part-time when his schedule allows him to be on the west coast where Stanford and her daughter now live.

Just weeks after Jackson attacked President-elect Bush and Attorney General-designate Ashcroft on their views and legitimacy, Jackson swings and misses embarrassing him and what's left of the civil rights movement in America.

Why is this man still trusted in so many circles? You remember Jackson calling then referring to New York as a "Hymie Town" in reference to the city's heavy Jewish population. There was uproar, but Jesse survived thanks to a liberal media and a Democratic Party without a moral or ethical compass.

Now this latest tidbit spews to the surface. Will Jackson be forever banished from public life? Nah.

In a prophetic twist, Jackson, speaking to Clinton at the height of his "open zipper" catastrophe, told Clinton, "The nation must take the test: If there are any among us who have not known the trials and tribulations and temptations, then throw a rock."

Jackson was certainly speaking from experience.

It's time for people (are you listening liberal, mainstream media?) to leave this man be. Don't put him on camera; don't quote his nonsensical Don King-like messages. He is not a leader and he is not a role model. He is an embarrassment to his people and to America in general.

Instead, show your compassion to his young daughter who knows not about her media whore father and his inflammatory rhetoric. She deserves your prayers and forgiveness.

What does Jesse deserve?

Nothing.

When history is written 50 years from now, Jesse Jackson will be known more for what he failed to do rather than what he accomplished in his lifetime. I just hope another leader emerges who has substance to go along with the flash.

TWENTY THREE

Florida - You are the Weakest Link, Goodbye!

The first account I heard of voter confusion in Palm Beach County, Florida, I laughed it off as rubbish. How could grown adults be confused by something as simple as a ballot?

Florida is home to Disneyworld and everything that goes with it in Orlando. That almost requires that I will visit in the next few years. With young kids and a wife with an addiction to anything Disney, I have no choice in the matter. But after watching the inhabitants of the Sunshine State struggle with a simple piece of paper and a punch-card ballot, I wonder how they even drive to work.

The first group to raise issue with the ballot was senior citizens. Apparently, the "complexity" of a simple ballot was a bit too much for the Ben Gay crowd. The infamous butterfly ballot was simple. An arrow pointed to the hole where you needed to punch your ballot. Insert the metal pen, and press. Even Coco the monkey could handle that. But apparently our senior citizens of Florida couldn't resulting in a massive amount of votes for Pat Buchanan. And here I thought they just liked old Pat in south Florida.

The next group to complain about the ballots was the black residents of Palm Beach. They claimed the confusion was racial related and enter Jesse. I still don't understand how a ballot can be racist but apparently some believed it could be.

Several great jokes made the e-mail rounds about the confusion in Florida. This one is related to punching ballots correctly:

Q: How many West Palm Beach voters does it take to screw in a light bulb?

A: Buchanan.

The ballot problems in Florida really did deserve to be made fun of. The exercise was ridiculous and comedians and everyday Americans alike were in a joking mood despite the seriousness of the issues at hand.

One of the issues raised in regard to Palm Beach County vote was the disproportionate amount for Pat Buchanan. Democrats used this high skewing number of votes for the militant Buchanan as a reason why the people deserved a revote and that there were truly voting irregularities in the county. This was the Democrat's rally cry for weeks and they still refer to it today.

In another case of irony for the Donkeys, soon after President Bush was inaugurated, allegations of Hillary Clinton promising presidential pardons for a Hassidic Jewish neighborhood's vote in her successful run for the New York senate seat she now fills. It appears the conservative neighborhood usually votes 90 percent Republican and did so in the primary for Rick Lazio. But in November, there was a complete turnaround and Hillary won 80 percent of the district. Weeks later, Bill Clinton pardoned for members of the neighborhood in prison for embezzlement. Sounds fishy and a bit familiar doesn't it?

I know that's New York and we're discussing Florida here but it shows, yet again, the Donkey's hypocrisy.

Of course, Florida became the nation's whipping boy and with good reason. How could one of the largest states in the Union be so backward and half-assed when it came to counting votes? I know for me it made me wonder how they count votes in Arkansas, Nebraska and smaller states like Maine. If Florida couldn't do it God knows who won the last three elections including McGovern's big loss in 1972. Maybe the nation's biggest liberal actually beat Nixon.

I got a million of them. Here's another Florida joke too good to pass up:

THE BALLOT COUNTING, ACCORDING TO DR. SEUSS:

Can we count them with our nose?
Can we count them with our toes?
Should we count them with a band?
Should we count them all by hand?
If I do not like the count,
I will simply throw them out!
I will not let this vote count stand,
I do not like them, and Al Gore I am!
Can we change these numbers here?
Can we change them, calm my fears?
What do you mean Dubya has won?
That is not fair! It ruins my fun!
Let's count them upside down this time
Let's count until the state is mine!
I will not let THIS vote count stand!
I do not like it, and AlGore I am!
I'm really ticked, I'm in a snit!
You have not heard the last of it!
I'll count the ballots one by one
And hold each up before the sun!
I'll count, recount, and count some more!
You'll grow to like this little chore!
I will not let this vote count stand!

I do not like it, and AlGore I am!
I won't leave office, stayin' here
I've glued my desk chair to my rear!
Tipper, Hillary, and Bubba too,
Are telling me that I should SUE!
"We find the Electoral College vile!
Recount the votes until WE smile!
We do not want this vote to stand!
We do not LIKE it, AlGore-I-am!"
How shall we count THIS ballot box?
Let's count it standing in our socks!
Shall we count this one in a tree?
And who shall count it, you or me?
We cannot, cannot count enough!
We must not stop, we must be tough!
I do not want this vote to stand!
I do not like it, and AlGore I am!
I've counted till my fingers bleed
and still can't fulfill my counting need.
I'll count the tiles on the floor
and even count the ones next door!
And I will not say I am done
until the counting says I've WON!
I will not let this vote count stand!
I do not like it, and AlGore I am!
What's that? What? What's that you say?
You think the current count should....STAY?????
You do not like my counting scheme?
It makes you tense? Gives you bad dreams?
Foolish folks, you're wrong, you'll see!
Your only care should be for ME!
I will not let this vote count stand!
I do not like it, and AlGore I am!

This clever joke and play on the popular Dr. Seuss

formula discusses another central issue on why Florida was

such a joke. When they did begin the doomed manual recounts, all 67 Florida counties had separate standard for counting those votes. In fact, several had no plans or standards on how to conduct manual recounts. The images of senior citizens holding up ballots and searching for dimpled chads will be indelibly marked in our national scrapbook to show what an utter waste of time the entire exercise was.

This was exemplified most when it hurt Al Gore. When the Florida Supreme Court ignored the U.S. Constitution for the second time and ordered a manual recount for the entire state, Gore looked as though he might come out the winner. But because most Florida counties spent the better part of two days arguing about how they would count votes and what votes they would count, time ran out and the Supreme Court of the United States shut down the Gore vote stealing machine.

Just around the time the election was finally coming to an end, the Florida Board of Tourism release this list of new slogans:

NEW SLOGANS FOR FLORIDA
FLORIDA: If you think we can't vote, wait 'till you see us drive.
FLORIDA: Home of electile dysfunction.

FLORIDA: We count more than you do.
FLORIDA: If you don't like the way we count, then take I-95 and visit one of
the other 56 states.
FLORIDA: We've been Gored by the bull of politics and we're Bushed.
FLORIDA: Relax, Retire, ReVote.
FLORIDA: Viagra voters do it again and again!
FLORIDA: Where your vote counts and counts and counts.
FLORIDA: This is what you get for taking Elian away from us.
FLORIDA: We're number one! Wait! Recount!
OR:
Palm Beach County: So nice, we let you vote twice.
Palm Beach County: We put the "duh" in Florida.
Sign on I-95 : Florida this way, no that way, 5 miles, wait 10 miles.

Of course these are more jokes. I just can't help but joke about Florida. We've all seen some pretty scary stories about crime in Florida. You can just about apply any joke about the rural South there too.

Don't get me wrong. There are great people in Florida. Including some I am related to. The fact remains, they didn't show their good side when it came to voting for president in 2000. I don't think it will hurt tourism but many people my age will have a lot of explaining to do when their kids and grandkids ask why they found it so hard to vote.

I appeared on the national *Nightsearch* radio show with Eddie Middleton on which I used some of my best Florida jokes. Soon after, I received this letter:

An Open Letter from the People Of Florida

OK, here's the deal. We here in Florida have all gotten together and decided to hold the rest of the country hostage with these here election results until you come and take your parents back home with you! That's right, we're tired of hearing how good it was back home and how beautiful your children are. We can't stand it any longer! And where did they learn to DRIVE????? We're running out of Depends down here and it's gonna get messy. You want a president ... We want the speed limit over 20 mph ... Is it a deal? George W, you listening? How about you, Mr. Gore? Ya gettin' this? We need a break, and quit sending the Canadians down here, too! We mean it, we're not lettin' the results out, we'll stall with lawsuits and claim ballot fraud. Anything until you come and take the old devils outta here!

Signed,
The People of Florida

I didn't think you'd take me seriously. Making fun of senior citizens isn't my idea of fun but I wanted to give a flavor of what the jokes of the day were. As Americans we've always been real good about making fun of ourselves and this time was no different. The television late night talk shows had the most fun with it and probably were the only segment of the population really disappointed the protracted event came to a close.

One last joke about Florida. The key to this one is singing it to the old kids song "The Hokey Pokey." Remember that one? If so sing this to that tune:

The Palm Beach Pokey

You put your stylus in,
You pull your stylus out,
You put your stylus in,
And you punch Buchanan out.
You do the Palm Beach Pokey
And you turn the count around,
That's what it's all about!
You put some Gore votes in,
You pull the Bush votes out,
You put some Gore votes in,
And you do another count.
You do the Palm Beach Pokey
And you turn the count around,
That's what it's all about!
You bring your lawyers in,
You drag the whole thing out,
You bring your lawyers in,
And you create lots of doubt.
You do the Palm Beach Pokey
And you turn the count around,
That's what it's all about!
You let your doctors spin,
You let the pundits spout,
You make the retirees sue,
And your people whine and pout.

You do the Palm Beach Pokey
And you turn the count around,
That's what it's all about!

Let's dispel with the jokes and get back to more serious post-election matters.

The one true positive for Florida is it will now be the breeding ground for true nationwide election reform. The problems we witnessed in Florida are really mirrored throughout the nation in many states. Not that it will be President Bush's top priority, but he should at some time during his eight year term push election reform on a national level by establishing universal guidelines for every county in every state.

The major issue with election reform will be the cost involved. Can a small county in South Dakota afford the most expensive voting system in the country? No. That's why the federal government will need to fund these initiatives and as a taxpayer I say we should send the money.

I'm not sure any members of Congress will read this book but if they do: SPEND THE MONEY!

TWENTY FOUR

The Great Law Breaker

I'd be remiss if I didn't at least devote some time to the outgoing president, William Jefferson Clinton.

Clinton's entire time in office can be summed up in what he did in leaving office on January 20, 2001. Here is how the Bill Clinton era ended:

- Phone lines in the White House were cut, rendering them inoperable.
- Voice mail messages were changed to obscene, scatological greetings. One Bush staffer had his grandmother call from the Midwest. She was horrified by what she heard on the other end of the line.
- Many phone lines misdirected to other government offices.
- Desks found turned completely upside down and trash deliberately left everywhere.

- Computer printers that were filled with blank paper but interspersed with pornographic pictures and obscene slogans that would be revealed only as items were run off the computer.
- 'W' keys weren't just pried off more than 40 keyboards, some were glued on with Superglue; some were turned upside down and glued on.
- Filing cabinets glued shut.
- VP Office space in the Old Executive Office Building found in complete shambles. Mrs. Gore had to phone Mrs. Cheney to apologize.
- Lewd Magic Marker graffiti found on one office hallway.

Yep. Clinton left office with his spoiled brat staffers defacing federal property. The complete lack of respect shown by Clinton and his immature staff was the final insult to the American people.

Oh, there was one more.

When Clinton made his final journey from Washington to his New York home, President Bush was gracious enough to allow him one more flight on Air Force One – an honor not afforded every outgoing president.

As he, Hillary and Chelsea left Air Force One, this is what Clinton and his staff were doing:

1.) The Washington Times reported that Air Force One was "stripped bare" during the former president's "official" farewell flight to New York on Inauguration Day.

2.) All the plane's porcelain china, silverware, salt and pepper shakers, blankets and pillow cases — most of it bearing the presidential seal — were taken by Clinton staff.

Those last incidents, when he had officially lost the office he so corrupted and tarnished, Clinton led the first presidential looting trip in history.

Thanks Bill. Here's wishing you – well, my mother always did say "If you don't have something nice to say, say nothing at all."

Bill Clinton = national embarrassment

The Bush Years Begin

TWENTY FIVE

The Bush Era – Chapter II

On January 20, 2001, George Walker Bush was sworn in as the 43rd President of the United States ending the election controversy that had waged for 36 days. As the rain fell that day in Washington, seemingly clensing gthe nation after the protracted presidential odysse, the traditional inaugural parade slowly made its way to the White House with a small amount of protests erupting along the route. Leftist Democratic fringe groups refused to accept, again, the results of the election and attempted to get close enough to Bush to burn him in efigee.

Luckily for America, the threats of violence and rowdy demonstrations marked the first time the Secret Service was in complete control of the day's activities and everything went off pretty well.

But after the parade was over, and after the balls and dancing, George W. Bush had much work to do. He inheirited a nation on the verge of a recession and an country still divided over the election and the fundamental differences between the two parties.

Looking forward, there are several key issues Bush will have to face during the first term of his presidency. Those issues include not only his political opposition within the country, but troubling developments on the international front related to a resurgent and hostile Russia and the ever-present threat of China. These two issues will perhaps dominate Bush's first term despite his domestic initiatives included his across the board tax cuts.

The Ashcroft Smokescreen

Because Democrats were still steaming over the loss of the close election, their first target and attempt to delegitimize Bush before he was sworn in was by attacking his cabinet appointments. Since Bush prevailed and Democrats would be forced to deal with a Republican for four to eight years, they were eager to shed some blood and take out their own frustrations on Bush and his readying administration.

The announcement of the appointment of former Missouri Governor Robert Ashcroft was met by outright viciousness by the party faithful for the Donkeys. Ashcroft's conservative record and personally religious views disturbed just about every group who sets up camp on the left. So called women's groups hated him, the NAACP hated him, the Democrats in the senate hated him and just about every group on the fringe decided it was Republican hinting season and Ashcroft was in the crosshairs.

Cogresswoman Maxine Watters, who loves Fidel Castrol and categorizes every conservative a "rascist", called Ashcroft a racist on national television. Jesse Jackson, while apparently paying hush money to his side honey, equated Ashcroft's nomination to Hitler's Germany of the 1930s. The National Organization of Women came right out and said he wouldn't protect Roe v. Wade and work to diminish laws that protect abortion.

All these groups. All of these camera whores pining for time to slam Ashcroft and label him a racist. If not a racist, then be "insensitive". In today's sensitive world, being labled "insensitive" implies racism but requires no proof. It's a sort of racism loop hole.

The problem with Ashcroft's detractors is they have never shown, nor did they offer, any proof that anything

Ashcroft has ever done or said is racist or that anything he has ever done professional borders on racism or racial "insensitivity."

The main support Ashcroft haters use to show is desire to hurt minorities was the case of Missouri Supreme Court Justice Ronnie White. White, who was appointed by Clinton to serve at the federal district court level, was not confirmed by Ashcroft while a member of congress. Adding fuel to the fire was Ashcroft's leadership in denying White his dream. Ashcroft lead the effort to deny White his position and this is why the Donkeys started leveling racial allegations at Ashcroft.

Ashcroft's reasoning was simple: he felt White was soft on crime and didn't appove of his appointment. It had nothing to do with race. But Watters, Jackson, the NAACP and other oganizations used the White case to show how "insensitive" Ashcroft was with a black appointee.

Left out of the argument was the fact Ashcroft voted to approved 25 out of 27 blacks who were nominated during his time in the senate. Add to that the fact Ashcroft was opposed to White due to a legal case in Missouri where White agreed to set free a violent murderer, who happened to be white, against the wishes of all police organizations, the governor's office and local politicians. Ashcroft came to the conclusion that White was not being hard enough on criminals thereby giving them an extra shot when one might have not been warranted.

So the fact Ashcroft, angry over the fact a white murderer was handled with kid gloves, fought against the judge who set him free is a racist move? If so, explain because there's nothing here folks.

In the end, the Donkeys were left to complain as Ashcroft won easy approval and was confirmed Attorney General of the United States. So Maxine; go live in Cuba with Fidel, no running water and starving people.

TWENTY SIX

The Bear on Bush's Watch

During the eight years of the Clinton administration, Russia was afforded every possible perk available to a foreign nation. Billions of dollars in aid were poured into the fledgling democracy by an administration willing to look past the 73 years of Communist rule in an effort to help promote democracy. In many ways, Russia became the 51st state receiving in many cases more federal aid than most of the states here at home. The idea was to keep democracy alive in the former Soviet Union by financing the conversation of the country's economic system and continued support of democratic political reforms.

The problem is the money was dumped into the lap of wealthy Russians who used it to line their own pockets while most people in Russia continued to fend off starvation and poverty. Add in the massive growth of the Russian mafia with the influx of American dollars and practically noting was accomplished in trying to change Russia from its once evil self.

Russia has missed several of its foreign debt payments and probably will default on billions of dollars in U.S. aid shelled out during Bubba's term in office.

Bush now inheirits a Russian policy as full of holes as Tupac Shakur. Russia's diabolical president Vladimir Putin continues to increase his anti-American rhetoric and has issued a challenge to the new administration warning against the development of a missile defense system telling the Canadian press in January of 2001 "If the Bush administration moves forward with their plans for a missile defense system, that may trigger another arms race larger than the Cold War."

Many inside Russia claim Putin is against the American missile defense system because it will most likely create another arms race. That would require Russia to spend more and more money just to keep up. Ultimately, Putin cannot afford a protracted arms race that could result in another economic collapse and perhaps the end of his political career.

Russia has completely snowed the world in thinking they were hurting economically during the preceeding era of political reform. Throughout the 1990s we were spoon-fed reports of Russia's deterioriating military infrastructure including the deterioration of the nuclear aresenal said to be at the point of complete disarray. The facts reveal a massive and well-hid build-up within the Russian military marking the largest expansion of the Russian fighting force since the late 1970s. This has prompted many to wonder just what plans Russia has for the new century. Will the Soviet Union rise again under Putin and what does that mean for a weakened U.S. military?

Under Putin, who was widely promoted by Clinton and Gore as a champion of democracy, Russia is rapidly moving toward a domestic dictatorship and the resurgence of the Soviet-type influence and world domination. Putin has dispatched his foreign emissaries to create strategic alliances with Iran and other Middle Eastern countries to reengage them to help Russia rise from the ashes of their perverted democracy experiment.

Putin has been working tirelessly since taking power to establish a strategic alliance with China and has been in discussions with nation's like India who harbor strong anti-

American feelings. This courting of anti-American nations should alarm the Bush administration and also warn America military spending must be increased to keep the peace and protect America's borders.

Perhaps most worrisome is Putin's decision to redeploy tactical nuclear weapons near Kaliningrad which marks a disturbing and unprecedented shift in Russian policy in the post-Communist era.

In addition, Russia continues to warm up to Red China and as of February 2001, was selling the Chinese nuclear missile technology. This new alliance exemplifies how fearful Russia is at the spectre of a new U.S. president who feels strongly about defending the United States.

Russia is a central issue for Bush as he settles into the recently scrubbed Oval Office. Bush must set a Russian policy early and it must be strong. The idea Russia will truly adopt democracy and continue down the road as a friendly nation is both naïve and poses a danger to the security of the United States. The sleeping bear is awaking and could come back stronger than ever.

The liberal left and its globalization initative could back Bush into a corner in which he might need to emerge swinging.

The wild card with Bush and Russian policy may be his Secretary of State Colin Powell. Powell has shown an increasing hostility toward Israel but hasn't come out strong against Russia begging the question what will be the Bush administration's policy toward the angry Putin and the growing Russian threat?

Many conservatives in the United States are worried about Bush primarily due to his seemingly blind trust in his newly established cabinet which include the aforementioned Powell. Many believe Powell is a loyal "New World Order" soldier looking to continue Clinton's role as the internal Globalist. Toss in the vice president Dick Cheney and many on the far right are concerned Bush may not be his own man when it comes to foreign policy. His lack of experience in the foreign relations arena hurt him on the campaign trail and many believe he will lean on Powell and Cheney to set policy.

I believe Bush will find a happy medium.

The idea that he is aloof and not too bright was a concoction of the media who refused to give Bush any personal credit for both his terms in Texas and his eventual ascension to the presidency.

Certainly Bush will lean on Powell and Cheney; with their combined experience he'd be both stupid and naïve not to. Are we forgetting why you name people such as Powell and Cheney to your cabinet in the first place?

Bush must establish early, which I feel he has, that he is in charge and even though he lacks the foreign policy experience his two most trusted cabinet members indeed have, he must lay down the law and do what he thinks is right. In relation to Russia, Bush will be tested. He will be tested and he'd better score well because Russia is on the rise and they are not looking to be a democracy too much longer. The odds are against it and if they laid a line in Las Vegas on whether or not the hard line Communists will rule again, I'd have to say it would be about 7-5 odds.

That's not good and Bush needs to accelerate his plans to rebuild the fighting force of America to meet the challenge. In addition, the further development of the missle defense system is a top priority for Bush and should be carried out no matter who complains about it.

If I had to guess, I would say we are at the dawn of a new Cold War with Russia. A Cold War that will result in another mini arms race in which I believe America can win again. If Bush enacts some of the same policies as Ronald Regan did during the early 1980s, Russia will again be driven to bankruptcy and on the verge of internal strife.

TWENTY SEVEN

Look Over Your Shoulder – Here Comes China

What will George W. Bush do about China? Since Clinton and Gore were in the bag for the Chinese, does that mean they will come to Bush wil the same unethical and illegal deals Clinton spent with them?

Bill Clinton was closer to China than Taiwan. Never has an American leader so embraced a nation whose main purpose it is to destroy our way of life. Clinton and Gore both accepted campaign contributions from wealthy Chinese looking to influence. Add in a lack of security at many of our top secret sites and you can imagine the leg up they now have on us. Whether it was nuclear secrets missing from Los Alamos or Al Gore's fundraising efforts, the Red Army had a special place in Clinton's cold and empty heart.

Bush must now figure a way to delicately balance diplomacy while at the same time exuding strength and resolve with the Chinese. If not, he could lose more respect and America could be hurt by a perceived weakness or willingness to continue the fight against Communism.

What's disturbing about China as Bush assumes office is its own massive arms build up. That coupled with recent threats against Taiwan, mean an escalating situation Bush will need to deal with soon. It's no a foreign relations issue left to Powell. Instead, Bush must step forward and challenge China to live as we do.

In his book, *A Promise to Keep*, Bush discusses briefly trade with China and thinks it's a good thing. And, for the American economy, it is. But Bush must be careful and more diligent than Clinton when dealing with the Chinese. China's aggression toward Taiwain is escalating and only weeks after Bush's inauguration, they moved more missiles and pointed them toward the island nation. This troublesome escalation in its Taiwan policy mirrors the aggression currently being seen with the Russians. It's as if they both are moving on concert with the threat of a Republican administration and a stronger U.S. military on the horizon.

Pushing against Bush is his own policy on free trade with China. Bush will be pressured to keep the markets flowing into China and to continue to mark the Communist nation as a top trade partner with the United State.

Bush has said on many occasions that China's threat to America is very real and that he will work to build our military and send a clear message to China that the United States will not stand for aggression against it or Taiwan. This, coupled with Bush's early push at a missile defense system, has riled the feathers of the Chinese and may be one of the reasons they are pushing more missiles towards their coast aimed at Taiwan.

Epilogue

Whether or not this book touches you or you agree with it, it's an actual account and collection of opinions by an everyday American who found himself entangled in perhaps the most historic event in presidential election history. I'm no award winning author or a scholar in search of the historical importance of the battle for Florida.

I'm just a working stiff like the rest of you who lived and breathed the election for every one of its 36 grueling days.

It was a time of optimism and fear.

A time when I felt the very foundation our nation was founded upon was almost destroyed buy power hungry politicians bent on winning at all costs.

Historians and scholars will look back at that period in American history and find two different places. Depending on which way that particular historian sways, you'll either read how justice prevailed or how voters were silenced because their votes were never counted.

You've gotten through this book so you know my view. I don't expect everyone to agree with my point of view. I may come across less than compassionate and a bit harsh to some of you. I understand that but this election was a battle to me. I had two small children at the time and the world they would inherit depended on actions today. I felt such a sense of responsibility for our nation and for our children that I became somewhat fanatical. But because I was fanatical, I didn't lose my reason and I never yelled or screamed at anyone, even that woman in the grocery store.

No matter what your view of what America should be, we all need to be involved in the political process. That includes reading daily and keeping on top of what our elected officials are doing. We need to make sure they are keeping America secure and not selling nights in the White House to Chinese businessmen. We need to constantly educate ourselves and keep them honest in Washington.

I hope that when my children read this book during their college years or when they have their own family history looks positively on George W. Bush. I think history will show he united a country severely divided on fundamental issues important to us all. Whether or not he is remembered as one of our finest presidents really doesn't matter. What matters most is at a time when we needed a man of wisdom, a man of compassion and a man of honor, he stepped forward and led a nation at war with itself.

Alexis and Ryan Gulbransen, it's your turn to write the next chapter in U.S. history. I hope when you're reading this sometime in the future, we've left you something worth fighting for – just as we did in the year of the broken election.

* * *

INDEX

About the Author

Scott Gulbransen is a former print journalist and current public realtions professional for one of America's top software companies. *The Broken Election* was his first book.

Gulbransen has extensive experience as both a writer and broadcaster hosting local and national radio programs and providing college football coverage for *USA Today*'s online division during the 1990s.

He is a graduate of the University of Nevada, Las Vegas where he earned his Bachelor's Degree in Communications with an outside emphasis in Political Science. Gulbransen, the married father of two, currently resides in San Diego, California.